Stephan Siehl

Electronic Commerce over Multiple Platforms

A European Study in the Use of eCommerce

Stephan Siehl

# Electronic Commerce over Multiple Platforms

**A European Study in the Use of eCommerce**

diplom.de

**Bibliografische Information der Deutschen Nationalbibliothek:**

Bibliografische Information der Deutschen Nationalbibliothek: Die Deutsche Bibliothek verzeichnet diese Publikation in der Deutschen Nationalbibliografie; detaillierte bibliografische Daten sind im Internet über http://dnb.d-nb.de/ abrufbar.

Copyright © 1999 Diplomica Verlag GmbH
Druck und Bindung: Books on Demand GmbH, Norderstedt Germany
ISBN: 978-3-8386-1991-0

http://www.diplom.de/e-book/217834/electronic-commerce-over-multiple-platforms

Stephan Siehl

# Electronic Commerce
# over Multiple Platforms
*A European Study in the Use of eCommerce*

**Diplomarbeit
an der Humboldt-Universität Berlin
Wirtschaftwissenschaftliche Fakultät
Prüfer Prof. Dr. Oliver Günther
August 1999 Abgabe**

***Diplomarbeiten* Agentur**
**Dipl. Kfm. Dipl. Hdl. Björn Bedey
Dipl. Wi.-Ing. Martin Haschke
und Guido Meyer GbR**

**Hermannstal 119 k
22119 Hamburg**

agentur@diplom.de
**www.diplom.de**

ID 1991
Siehl, Stephan: Electronic Commerce over Multiple Platforms: A European Study in the
Use of eCommerce / Stephan Siehl · Hamburg: Diplomarbeiten Agentur, 1999
Zugl.: Berlin, Universität, Diplom, 1999

Dipl. Kfm. Dipl. Hdl. Björn Bedey, Dipl. Wi.-Ing. Martin Haschke & Guido Meyer GbR
Diplomarbeiten Agentur, http://www.diplom.de, Hamburg
Printed in Germany

**Diplomarbeiten** Agentur

# Wissensquellen gewinnbringend nutzen

**Qualität, Praxisrelevanz und Aktualität** zeichnen unsere Studien aus. Wir bieten Ihnen im Auftrag unserer Autorinnen und Autoren Wirtschafts-studien und wissenschaftliche Abschlussarbeiten – Dissertationen, Diplomarbeiten, Magisterarbeiten, Staatsexamensarbeiten und Studien-arbeiten zum Kauf. Sie wurden an deutschen Universitäten, Fachhoch-schulen, Akademien oder vergleichbaren Institutionen der Europäischen Union geschrieben. Der Notendurchschnitt liegt bei 1,5.

**Wettbewerbsvorteile verschaffen** – Vergleichen Sie den Preis unserer Studien mit den Honoraren externer Berater. Um dieses Wissen selbst zusammenzutragen, müssten Sie viel Zeit und Geld aufbringen.

**http://www.diplom.de** bietet Ihnen unser vollständiges Lieferprogramm mit mehreren tausend Studien im Internet. Neben dem Online-Katalog und der Online-Suchmaschine für Ihre Recherche steht Ihnen auch eine Online-Bestellfunktion zur Verfügung. Inhaltliche Zusammenfassungen und Inhaltsverzeichnisse zu jeder Studie sind im Internet einsehbar.

**Individueller Service** – Gerne senden wir Ihnen auch unseren Papier-katalog zu. Bitte fordern Sie Ihr individuelles Exemplar bei uns an. Für Fragen, Anregungen und individuelle Anfragen stehen wir Ihnen gerne zur Verfügung. Wir freuen uns auf eine gute Zusammenarbeit

### Ihr Team der *Diplomarbeiten* Agentur

Dipl. Kfm. Dipl. Hdl. Björn Bedey –
Dipl. Wi.-Ing. Martin Haschke ——
und Guido Meyer GbR ————

Hermannstal 119 k ——————
22119 Hamburg ——————

Fon: 040 / 655 99 20 —————
Fax: 040 / 655 99 222 ————

agentur@diplom.de ——————
www.diplom.de ——————

# Acknowledgements

Thank you Inca Lork for her advise in spelling and habits of the English language. Thank you Olaf Dörge for his constructive criticism and advise during this work.

A special thank you to Eric Dalström from Hyperion who let this project become possible and woke the desire in me to deal with Electronic Commerce in the future.

Berlin, 1 August 1999

# Contents

3

# Abbreviations

| | |
|---|---|
| ADSL | Asymmetrical Digital Subscriber Line |
| API | Application Programming Interface |
| ATM | Asynchronous Transfer Mode |
| a.o. | among others |
| CREC | Center for Research in Electronic Commerce UT Austin |
| Cf. | Consider following |
| CI | Common Interface |
| DMS | Document Management Systems |
| DTV | Digital TV |
| DVB | Digital Video Broadcasting |
| EC | Electronic Commerce |
| Ed. | Editor |
| EDI | Electronic Data Interchange |
| EDIFACT | Electronic Data Interchange for Administration, Commerce and Transport |
| EFT | Electronic Funds Transfer |
| EU | European Union |
| F.U.N. | Free Universe Network |
| GPRS | General Packet Radio Service |
| GSM | Groupe Speciale Mobile |
| GVU | Graphics, Visualisation & Usability |
| HDTV | High Digital TV |
| HSCSD | High Speed Circuit Switched Data |
| IP | Internet Protocol |
| ISDN | Integrated Services Digital Network |
| NSF | National Science Foundation |
| PAP | Public Access Points |
| SDTV | Standard Digital TV |
| SGML | Standard Generalised Markup Language |
| VAN | Value Added Network |

| | |
|---|---|
| WAP | Wireless Application Protocol |
| WFM | Work Flow Management |
| WWW | World Wide Web |
| XML | Extended Markup Language |

# Figures

# Tables

# 0 Introduction

Never before has an information technology generated so much media coverage, and so much interest, as the Internet. For example, radio took 38 years to get 50 million users. TV took 13 years to get 50 million. PC took 13 years. The Internet took 4 years [BRA99, p.6].

"Sitting on top of the Internet is electronic commerce. The e-commerce marketplace is now the fastest growing part of the world economy. Worth $12 billion/11 billion ecu in 1997, it is forecast to grow to around $350/321 ecu to $500/458 billion ecu[1] by 2002" [BRA99, p.6]. Its importance for the future economy can be estimated by 'sky-rocking' stock-quotes of companies operating in the business of Electronic Commerce (EC). In the beginning, EC-solutions were developed and sold by small, innovative and specialised companies. Today the major players in the computer, tele-phone or media business are working overtime to reposition themselves to catch up with the extreme fast development of EC. For example, Microsoft, the major player in the business-software section, is aggressively moving towards an integrated service network, containing the software, the transmitting medium and the content, by buying mid-size start-up companies and creating strategic alliances.

In this context, this study is focused in the way, in which people access the Internet in future for information, shopping, leisure, etc.. In this future access-way: "Increasingly, consumers are demanding web-based access to goods and services, and this demand is set to explode as internet access extends to TVs, mobile phones and other personal devices" [SPO99, p.12]. These access-devices are understood as EC platforms in this context. This study will show that the PC will loose its position as *the* only access-medium to services or products via the Internet.

The future question is not if EC will change our daily lives but how it will change it. The trend towards a more user orientated way to provide content, in which techno-logical skills become less important, has begun. In the future, EC will be executed (besides PCs) via specialised, easy to use devices.

---

[1] The Euro is meant in this case.

This study, as part of an European research project, will cover the German EC market. Different access platforms, its penetrations and possible future developments will be analysed.

This work is structured in 3 parts: Firstly, the theoretical framework in which the EC platforms are positioned. Secondly, the German position within Europe and in contrast to US concerning internet-use and EC are analysed. Two surveys were undertaken and combined with secondary data found in the literature to get a concise picture. Thirdly, the study is concluded by two case-studies, presenting different access-platforms in detail.

In chapter 1 the fundament for this work will be laid by outlining the subject of Electronic Commerce (EC). Chapter 1.1 defines EC and establishes an 'working-hypothesis' for this work. Afterwards the underlying power of EC - the reduction of Transaction Costs - will be discussed and the theory described in brief. Chapter 1.3 gives a brief overview of the EC history and in chapter 1.4 the platforms will be put into a general framework of EC. After describing the barriers and drivers for EC in chapter 1.5, the four different platforms computer, mobile phone, Digital TV and Public Access Point will be described in chapter 2 and its features discussed. Chapter 3 deals with EC, focused especially on German market, comparing it with Europe or/and the US. The first section of chapter 3 is divided into EC volume, infrastructure and use. The second part analyses two surveys carried out during this work, both were especially focused on the topic EC platforms, because in the literature at present this aspect is not covered sufficiently. Chapter 3.4 analyses an expert questionnaire ran during the Internet World (faire) in Berlin and via e-mailing to company representatives involved in EC. Chapter 3.5 describes the results of a general questionnaire undertaken from March to July 1999 via e-mailing, a web-page and personal interviews. Its aim was to get an impression of the status in which Germany is at present concerning EC. The study is concluded with two case-studies of platforms for EC, outlining the practical use of the theoretical described functionality and technological features of EC devices. A Digital TV receiver from Galaxis and ZDFs Electronic Program Guide, as well as a Public Access Point called T-Kiosk from Deutsche Telekom will be presented.

# 1 Electronic Commerce

## 1.1 Defining Electronic Commerce

Narrowly defined, electronic commerce (EC) means doing business online or selling and buying products and services through Web storefronts. Today the term EC has developed further from its meagre notion of electronic shopping, which now means that all aspects of business and market processes are made possible/available by the Internet and the World Wide Web (WWW) technologies. Along with online selling, EC will lead to significant changes in the way products are customised, distributed and exchanged and the way consumers search and bargain for products and services and consume them [CR99a]. EC's manifoldness yields to various definitions. From the many attempts to define EC, two will be presented next and a 'working-hypothesis' established. The first approach focuses on the characteristic of EC, whereas the latter describes the entities involved in possible EC transactions.

## 1.1.1 Defining Electronic Commerce by the Perspective

Kalakota and Whinston focus with their approach to establish a definition of EC on the aspect of the perspective from which it is seen. They show the complexity and the difficulty to commit one precise definition of EC by the following statements, which all are valid but focusing on different perspectives of EC [KRWA97,p.3].

> „From a *communications* perspective, EC is the delivery of information, products/services, or payments via telephone lines, computer networks, or any other means.
>
> From a *business process* perspective, EC is the application of technology towards the automation of business transactions and workflows.
>
> From a *service* perspective, EC is a tool that addresses the desire of firms, consumers and management to cut service costs while improving the quality of goods and increasing the speed of service delivery.
>
> From an *online* perspective, EC provides the capability of buying and selling products and information on the Internet and other online services."

All theses definitions point out different aspects of EC's potential to improve the execution of business transactions over various networks. These improvements may result in more effective performance (better quality, greater economic satisfaction and better corporate decision making), greater economic efficiency (lower costs), and more rapid exchange (high speed, accelerated, or real-time interaction).

The networks on which these interactions occur can be telephone lines (analogue or digital), cable TV, leased lines, wireless and electric lines[2] or combinations of them.

Next the second approach, which describes EC by the parties involved in the EC transaction-process will be outlined.

### 1.1.2 Defining Electronic Commerce by the Parties Involved

An other way to look at the aspect of EC is defined by the parties involved in the (online) transaction process. Four different scenarios are possible (see Figure 1):

*Figure 1 Transaction Scenarios*

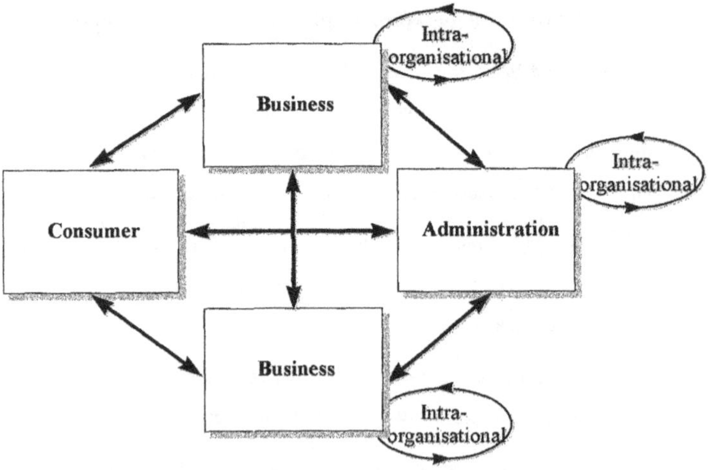

source: [TP99] with extensions

---

[2] RWE introduced an new system in march 1999, that implements internet-access via a special modem through the electric lines in households.

Keywords for the business-to-business scenario are EDI and supply-chain-management, which will be described in detail in chapter 1.3. The business-to-consumer scenario covers mainly aspects of electronic retailing, examples are online-shops like *amazon.com* or *primus.de*. The categories business-to-administration and consumer-to-administration contain transactions between corporations/consumers and administration. In the-business-to-administration sections for example are public invitations to tender via the Internet. An example for the consumer-to-administration category are the use of health-cards which reduced a lot of paperwork between health insurance companies and medical institutions.

Another aspect of EC, which is not mentioned by Timmers (source of Figure 1) are the intra-organisational transactions. These transactions can be summarised by the topics of Work Flow Management (WFM) and Document Management Systems (DMS), which had enormous growth-rates in the past.

Depending on the parties involved in the transaction process, different studies were carried out. Most consulting companies studies focus on the business perspective, using representative methodologies.[3] Other studies like the internet surveys form W3B or GVU (Graphics, Visualisation & Usability) from Georgia Tech Research Corporation are open surveys, which concentrate on the behaviour and the attitudes of consumers (internet-users).[4]

### 1.1.3 Establishing a 'Working-Hypothesis'

After describing two approaches to define EC, a 'working-hypothesis' will be established. As always, it is difficult to establish an intuitive, precise definition in a short manner, which takes all eventualities into account and is valid over the time. The same holds for the complex system of EC. As mentioned in the beginning of this chapter, the first approach tries to define EC by describing what it does, the second outlines who is using it.

---

[3] Good examples for these kind of studies are: [KPMG98] and [AC98].

[4] Abstracts of these studies can be found in [W3B99] and [GVU99].

To my opinion, the one definition is not complete without the other, because both handle only one side of the medal. Therefore, for this study the following definition which considers both aspects of EC will be established as a 'working-hypothesis':

*Electronic Commerce is the electronic delivery of information, products or services between different transaction-entities and/or within the organisation of these entities.*

After establishing a 'working-hypothesis' for this study, the underlying business-process improvement potential will be described in the next chapter.

## 1.2 Electronic Commerce and Transaction Costs

Why does EC embody the chance to improve business transactions? Wiliamson´s Transaction Cost Theory offers an explanation. His definition of a transaction is as follows: "A transaction occurs when a product or service is transferred across a technologically separable interface" [WIL85, p.112]. Transaction costs are defined as cost of information and communication. These cost can be caused through initiation, negotiation, control or adaptation.[5] When buyer/seller transactions occur in the electronic marketplace, information is accessed, absorbed, arranged and sold in different ways (see Figure 2)[6].

*Figure 2 Buyer-Seller Transaction*

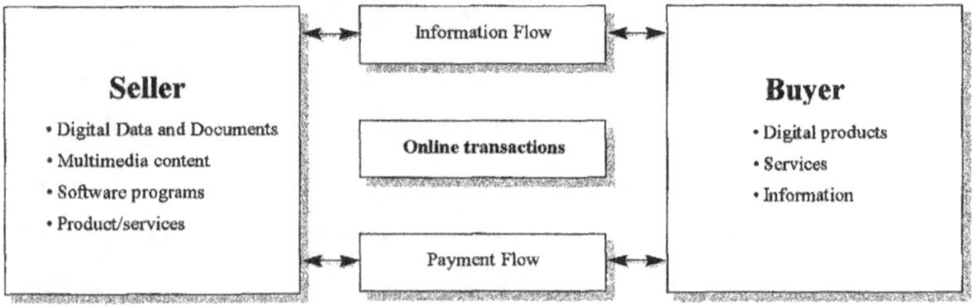

source: [KRWA97, p.4]

---

[5] A good overview of the Transaction Cost Theory can be found in: [PIC90, pp.178-184] and [PIC91, pp.154-150].

[6] The buyer/seller transaction represents a generalisation of the four different transaction-scenarios in the previous chapter.

To manage these transactions, EC incorporates transaction management, which organises, routes, processes and tracks transactions. This leads to a diminution of transaction costs and can result in more effectiveness (customer satisfaction through faster and better tailored service) or/and more efficiency (cost reduction) [PLI95, p.86].

EC also includes consumers making electronic payments and fund transfers. In connection with this, secure transactions become important. This will be described in more detail in Chapter 1.4.

Transactions don't always have to be carried out between two entities (buyer/seller). Intermediaries are often switched between a transaction. This intermediaries convert digital inputs to value-added outputs. For example, in the case of on-line trading, the stock quotes are expanded by charts, which represents an added value for the customer.

Currently, the goal of most EC research and its associated implementations is to reduce the 'friction' in on-line transactions. These 'frictions' are the transaction costs introduced above. By reducing transaction costs EC enables smoother transactions between buyers, intermediaries and sellers.

Kalokota and Whinston explain the powerful transaction-cost-reducing potential of EC by the simple intuitive equation: Profit = Revenue - Costs [KRWA97, p.5].

Revenue can be increased by:

- creating new markets for old products;

- creating new information-based products;

- establishing new service delivery channels to better serve and interact with the customer.

Operating costs can be reduced through:

- better co-ordination in the sales, production and distribution (or better supply-chain management);

- consolidation of operations;

- reduction of overhead.

## 1.3  From Traditional to Internet-Driven Electronic Commerce

EC is not a new phenomenon, its origins reach back to the 1960s, when IBM introduced its bisynchronous communication protocols (one-to-one basis) for the mainframe environments [KRWA99].

Business-centred EC began more than two decades ago during the 1970s, with the introduction of electronic funds transfers (EFT) between banks over secure private networks. This changed financial markets in as much as electronic fund transfers optimised electronic payments with electronically provided remittance information. Each day, over $4 trillion change hands via EFT over the computer networks linking banks, automated clearinghouses, and companies. The US Treasury Department estimates 55 percent of all payments by the federal government in 1995 were executed via EFT [KRWA99]. During the late 1970s and early 1980s, the use of EC became widespread within companies in the form of electronic messaging technologies: electronic data interchange (EDI) and electronic mail (sending and receiving order, delivery and payment information, etc.). In the late 1980s and early 1990s electronic messaging technologies became an integral part of workflow or collaborative computing systems (also called groupware). A prominent example of such a system is Lotus Notes.

Even consumer-orientated EC has a rather long history: each time automatic teller machines are used or credit cards are presented, business-transactions take place electronically. These EDI and Automatic Teller Machines, however, operate in a closed system; they are of a more convenient communications medium, strictly between the parties allowed in the network.

Setting up an EDI is expensive and therefore only large firms could justify in investing in EDI. Security-wise, in comparison to the Internet EDI offers robust transactions since it runs on closed, private networks. However, for this reason, the number of trading partners is always limited to those who are connected to these networks.

The emerge of the Internet in the mid-1980s became a turning point in EC. The Internet offered an open platform for new EC, removing the long lead times, asset specificity, and bilaterality of EC based on the traditional proprietary EDI. This was the basis for a cheaper way of doing business (economies of scale) and enabled more diverse business activities (economies of scope) [KRWA97, p.7]. The commercial use of the Internet, driven by its World Wide Web subset, has been defining a new kind of EC since 1993.[7]

EC now emerges from the convergence of several major information technologies and business practices. Amongst the principal technologies which directly enable modern EC are:

- computer networking and telecommunications;

- client/server computing;

- multimedia, and hypermedia in particular;

- information retrieval systems;

- electronic data interchange (EDI);

- message handling and workflow management systems;

- groupware and electronic meeting systems;

- and public key cryptography.

In a broader sense, all the major computer and telecommunication technologies, and database management in particular, undergird EC [ZWA99].

Kalakota and Whinston emphasises the aspect of syntax and semantics in the context of legal, accounting and auditing considerations. To them the future of EC depends on new forms of flexible EDI. Firstly because, these forms use a structured document language (e.g. SGML or XML) that communicates as clearly as the rigid EDI, to indicate the intent of transactions. The use of a structured document language provides a great deal of flexibility for post processing of forms in various down-stream business processes. This promises to eliminate the problems posed by the competing of vertical industries aligned, which are segregated by VAN's (Value Added Netwoks) that impede effective business process creation and management, due to their inflexibility. Secondly, because of the issues of privacy and security. New EDI implementations

---

[7] The World Wide Web, which has brought people to the Internet, was devised by Tim Berners-Lee in 1989 as a means of collaboration for the physicists working on the projects of the international research centre CERN. However, it is actually the first popular Web browser, NCSA Mosaic

enable companies to make secure EDI transactions over the Internet rather than through their VAN, which level per-character or per-message fees [KRWA99]. Examples of these new EDI implementations can be seen in Premenous Inc. Templar[8].

The use of the Internet for EC enables small companies to compete with resource-rich companies in a new manner. Competitive advantages become more and more a matter of quickness in which companies enter the market with superior products/services. These upstarts can enter the marketplace of several million customers with a minimal infrastructure investment: a PC, a modem, and an Internet account. For example, in web-based electronic trading, media giant Bertelsmann AG unveiled its online shop *Books Online* (bol) in France and Germany in February 1999. After *Amazon.com* established itself within 3 years from a small 'garage company' to the third-largest bookstore world-wide [WSJE99a].

## 1.4 A Framework for Electronic Commerce

To analyse the complex system of EC, a hierarchical framework similar to the ISO/OSI layer model is presented. As the ISO/OSI model, it consist of several hierarchical layers, which each of the lower ones delivering a well-defined functional support to the higher ones. The different layers (functions) and examples for them are displayed in Tab.1[9]. In the following the different layers of the framework are described in brief, as it merely serves to put in order the platforms of EC in a lager context.

### Technological Infrastructure: The Transportation-Level of EC Content

The first three layers (beginning from the bottom) of the framework are the *technological infrastructure* of EC. These layers are responsible for the transportation and presentation of the fundamental contents of EC - the information as a bit-stream. The transport takes place over wide-area-networks (WAN), extended by the metropolitan

---

(designed by Marc Andreessen, not much later a founder of Netscape) that began to bring people and businesses to the Web in the spring of 1993.

[8] Templar uses RSA Data's encryption method to wrap up EDI transmission in a secure 'mailer', which then can be sent by Internet E-mail. Templar is being tested by Cisco Systems Inc. and three of its trading partners .

(MAN) and local-area-networks (LAN). For this, guided (such as fibre-optic and co-axial cable) and wireless transmission media (such as microwave and the radio) under computerised control are being used. Above this layer the Internet and VAN`s are placed which are the principal vehicles for EC. The infrastructure level is completed by the WWW layer, the standard presentation application of the consumer EC contents.

*Tab. 1 The Hierarchical Framework of Electronic Commerce*

| Meta-Level | Functions | Examples |
|---|---|---|
| Products and Structures | Electronic Marketplaces and Electronic Hierarchies | • Electronic auctions, brokerages, dealerships, and direct search markets<br>• Interorganisational Supply-chain management |
| | Products and Systems | • Remote consumer services (retailing, banking, stock brokerage)<br>• Infotainment-on-demand (fee-based content sites, educational offering)<br>• Supplier-customer linkages<br>• On-line marketing<br>• Electronic benefit systems<br>• Intranet- and extranet-based collaboration |
| Services | Enabling Services | • Electronic catalogues/directories, smart agents<br>• E-money, smart-card systems<br>• Digital authentication services<br>• Digital libraries, copyright-protection services<br>• Traffic auditing |
| | Secure messaging | • EDI, EFT, E-mail |
| Infrastructure | Hypermedia/Multimedia Object Management | • World Wide Web with Java |
| | Public and Private Communication Utilities | • Internet and Value-added-networks (Van's) |
| | Wide-Area Telecommunication Infrastructure | • Guided- and wireless-media networks |

source: [ZWA99]

**Services: Enablers of Business Communication and Commerce**

---

[9] A similar framework is presented in [KRWA97, p.12].

The Service Level contains the Secure-Messaging- and Enabling-Services-Layer, which provides the business infrastructure for EC. Secure Messaging summarises attributes like confidentiality (generally accomplished through encryption), message integrity (achieved with tokens accompanying the message) and authentication of both parties (generally via digital signature and possession of a private key), which will be described in more detail in the next chapter. Some transactions require additional attributes, for example anonymity in conjunction with the generation of electronic cash (accomplished with a blinding factor during the encryption). As the Internet Protocol (IP) does not supply secure messaging attributes, they have to be provided on other layers. At present, different protocols are actively considered for various levels of communication, from the network to the application. A good example is the Secure Electronic Transaction (SET) protocol layer presented by VISA and MasterCard which enables secure credit card transactions over the Internet or Smart-Cards handling the authentication problem. As mentioned in the beginning of the chapter, the framework serves as a tool, to put in order platforms of EC in a broader context. Following this concept, a definition of EC platforms is presented next:

> *Different platforms for EC (for example mobile phones or Digital TV)*
> *are devices, using the functions of the Infrastructure Level (partly or*
> *complete) to enable functions of the Service Level. Platforms repre-*
> *sent the technological basis on which enabling services work.*

The most turbulent technological and entrepreneurial activity is taking place at the level of Enabling Services. When the previous layers built the necessary infrastructure and basic communication protocols for EC, this and the next layer(s) are the fundamental functions for EC. Keyword in this context are ebusiness, eEurope etc..[10] This level of EC includes for example digital libraries or Smart-Cards as well as research areas like electronic money and smart agents.

**Products and Structures: Applications of Electronic Commerce**

---

[10] IBM uses the term ebusiness for their EC-division [IBM99]; Andersen Consulting uses the term eEurobe as the headword for their EC Report [AC98].

The Products and Structures Level is covered by three categories of EC: consumer-orientated commerce, business-to-business commerce and intra-organisational commerce [ZWA99].

Consumer-orientated EC applications include for example home-shopping, banking and infotainment-on-demand accompanied by (and in some cases, so far paid by) on-line advertising. The potential of this marked segment can be estimated by the exploding stock marked capitalisation of companies like *Amazon.com* or *Yahoo*, targeting this segment. Another application for consumer-orientated EC can be government transfers over the Internet. For example, the Berlin government started the Information and Service page *Berlin.de*, where people will get actual information and have, among other things, the possibility to download tax forms and send in their tax returns [BER99].

The fastest growing area on the Products and Structures Level of EC is the intranet- and extranet-based information sharing and collaboration. Intranet-applications include working on compound documents or video conferencing. Extranets lead to an integrated supply-chain, linking suppliers/customers to the company (through EDI). The business-to-business section is the best established EC application, which claimed 65% of the EC marked in 1997 [ECI99] mainly with EDI. This category will further expand vastly by the growth of new EDI (open EDI).

The creation of integrated networks of multiple buyers and multiple suppliers let "traditional notations of hierarchical value chain collapse (as business partnerships change more frequently). Companies find themselves instead part of a much more dynamic marketplace, in which industry and corporate boundaries are less distinct. Companies will have to specialise even more on their distinctive roles within the new 'value network'" [AC98]. The change in the traditional value chain can be explained through the Market-Hierarchy Paradigm of the Transaction Cost Theory. The decrease of transaction costs leads to 'more market' in transactions, which were former executed hierarchically. Many and serious questions about the effects of EC on business governance are an area of further research needs [NSF99].

In the following these research-needs and estimated barriers/drivers for the users (companies) of EC will be presented.

## 1.5 Barriers and Drivers of Electronic Commerce

First of all the barriers perceived by the users and further research needs mentioned by the NSF (National Science Foundation) will be presented. Afterwards the main drivers named by company representatives in two Electronic Commerce Research Reports will be discussed.

### 1.5.1 Barriers: Perceived Issues and Topics of Further Research

When talking about barriers of EC one has to distinguish between perceived barriers of users (companies/consumers) and aspects in EC that need further research from a scientivic view. Often, distinguished threats of EC perceived by users are already solved but the adoption of these new technologies solving earlier problems is limping. An Example is the credit-card payment over the internet, only a few users are informed about SET or Smart-Cards. Most of the former technological barriers are solved at that stage but more general terms of interactions between users become potential barriers. In this context economical, psychological and legal questions arise. First the former technological barriers and their solutions are described in brief, afterwards the new arising barriers are outlined.

**Barriers: Perceived Issues**

Most of the former technological barriers can be described as *internet security problems*. These terms are [KRWA97, p.124]:

- *Authentication*: the transactions parties are who they say they are. A way of verification are digital signatures provided by smart-cards.

- *Integrity*: the information can not be manipulated. This is guaranteed through encryption technologies like Netscape's Secure Socket Layer or Secure HTML.

- *Reliability*: the system will perform consistently and at an acceptable level of quality. It is tried to guarantee through powerful infrastructure (high performance server, redundancy, etc) but it remains a serious (financial) problem, as exploding EC will require enormous infrastructure challenges over the next 5 years. Forrester Research estimates that running a 99,99%

available midrange EC system costs $6.9 million to buy and $2.9 million per year to run in the US. Therefore Forrester Research suggests that only EC leaders should build non-stop EC systems in-house, the other companies should outsource their systems [FOR99].

- *Encryption*: making information indecipherable except to those with the decoding key. An approved encryption method is the RSA public key algorithm which consists of a private and a public key, making the transactions convenient.

- *Data-protection*: keeping corporate networks secure from forbidden access but allowing authenticated users uninhibited access to the Internet. A way to protect company's servers are proxy servers (Firewalls), sitting between Internet and the company.

With the emerge of EC to the general public, specific transaction security issues became important. For Kalakota and Whinston five *internet security requirements* are imperative for the widespread acceptance of EC. These terms are privacy (of information/transaction), authenticity (of the transacting entities), integrity (of stored/transacted information), availability (of information) and blocking (of information (for example in the payment-process)) [KRWA97, p.135]. Although mostly solved, the security and privacy issues are the most important (perceived) EC barriers to the users. To get an impression of the most relevant aspects, excerpts of surveys from KPMG's and Andersen Consulting's (AC) annual EC Research Reports are presented in the following [AC98] [KPMG98]. Andersen Consulting interviewed 321 senior executives of European (291) and US (30) companies about general barriers of EC; KPMG interviewed marketing directors of 500 European companies with an annual turnover above $150 million about potential implementation barriers of EC.

AC found that most significant barriers of EC are concerns of security and privacy that arise from online transactions (see Figure 3 next page). For example, 61% of the total respondents mentioned lack in security of financial details, 59% mentioned concern about privacy of transaction a 'total barrier'. Interesting is that the themes (lack of) regulatory framework and lack of appropriate culture nationality are seen as relatively low barriers (39% and 29%) which indicates a view that leaves the development of EC to the private sector.

*Figure 3  Potential Barriers of Electronic Commerce*

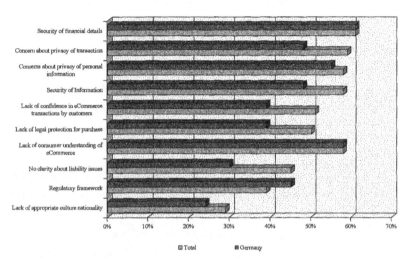

source: [AC98, p.31]

KPMG found that 25% of the respondents  see security and 24% lack of potential customers connected to the Internet as an implementation barrier. KPMG sees security as an 'overhyped' concern because tools for overcoming security risks are available. On the other hand the lack of customers connected is seen as a serious barrier which shows the need of more widespread internet access availability (through new platforms). Other aspects like costs or lack of knowledge are only seen by 10% or less of the respondents as an implementation-barrier [KPMG98, pp16].

After describing the early technological barriers which are still perceived as barriers of EC by the users in some part, in the following further research needs mentioned by the National Science Foundation (NSF) in its NSF Workshop - Research Priorities in Electronic Commerce [NSF99] are presented in brief. These research efforts/needs are the general questions arising from EC mentioned in the beginning of this chapter. If unsolved, these needs can become serious barriers for EC.

**Barriers: Topics of Further Research**

Because EC will have fundamental effects on various areas of personal or institutional interaction (e.g. business, social or psychological) the NSF workshop recommends an interdisciplinary research approach and points out the need for "defining and identifying characteristics and principals of a new economic system" [NSF99, Executive Summary]. In addition the paper calls for a more active role and leadership of the public sectors, which are government and the stakeholders in the basic research community such as the NSF. This is justified by the public-good characteristics of networks, information, digital products and the peculiarities of spaceless, contactless markets that bring about potential market failures.[11]

The NSF workshop focused on three different aspects of EC and outlined the respective current research efforts and critical research needs. The different aspects are especially: *System Architecture, Privacy, Security and Organisational Changes* and *Refinement in Basic Economic and Scientific Principles.*

*System Architecture*

Current research efforts are security and reliability in transactions, web-searching and net-centric, component-based technologies. These named efforts are mainly technology based attempts which created already various solutions. Critical research needs of system architecture remain [NSF99, 3.2]:

- negotiation contracts and agents;
- human-computer interaction;
- support of remote and real-time-interaction;
- EC measurement.

In the context of multiple platforms of EC the research of human-computer interaction is of central importance. Current research activities are focused on developing natural, easy to use interfaces based on multimedia presentation, speech and voice recognition technologies, vision I/O, 3-D and virtual reality. "Critical issues in human-

---

[11] In the economic theory these market failures are described by the asymmetric information of the transaction entities.

computer interface design include multi-modal interfaces in the face of converging communication technologies, and the need to separate content from presentation logic in order to assure consistency and efficiency" [NSF99, 3.2] An approach to separate content from presentation are SGML or XML.[12]

*Privacy, Security and Organisational Changes*

Privacy and security are of fundamental consumer interest but the marketplace does not have incentives to support such interests. This potential market failures are caused through under-investment of the private sector and the public-good aspects of some EC products. Current security research-focus has shown that: Inadequate technology to support EC, inadequate risk management models through technology driven solutions and no agreement upon information assurance standards exist and therefore further research is necessary. The same holds for the research in social and organisational systems, where research is still in the early beginning.

These specific research issues raised include [NSF99, 4.2]:

- theoretical justification of proposed business models;
- unbundling the concept of trust from interdisciplinary perspective and characterise it quantitatively;
- identification of models that address the layering of security mechanism to protect information;
- jurisdiction and conflicts of policy and law issues;
- economic analysis of legal rules pertaining to risk allocation.

*Refinements in Basic Economic and Scientific Principles*

The NSF states that "currently, economic and social scientists are only beginning to pay attention to potential effects of digital technologies on their areas of interest" [NSF99, 5]. Important research issues in this context are electronic markets, digital

---

[12] The advantage of XML in contrast to HTML is the definition of markup tags that describe the context of the document. This enables search-engines and agents to 'understand' and not only present a document.

commodities and incentive (of) compatible mechanism design. Of particular interest in connection with electronic markets are the uncertainty-problem (asymmetric information) and the pricing of digital commodities, as some of them have public-good characteristics. Further research is needed in the field incentive compatible mechanism design, as a truly global economic system with worldwide stresses, contributions and interdependency will overstrain our tools, analytic abilities and data sources. The impacts on the global economy requires particular considerations about the efficient handling of future Knowledge Markets. These mechanisms include [NSF99, 5.3]:

- bounded resources handling;
- complexity handling;
- the customisation of environments;
- the choice for a specific environment;
- competition (among mechanisms);
- design for resource allocation problems.

Although computer and engineering science have laid the foundation for EC, further interdisciplinary, systematic research activities are needed to generate necessary knowledge and methods to maximise their potential.

### 1.5.2 Drivers: Accelerators of Electronic Commerce

Drivers of EC are applications, hardware or infrastructure innovations that accelerate the development and adoption of EC. Each of these areas are subjects of intensive researches by scientists and companies involved in the EC and internet-business. As the subject of this (empirical) study is to outline the use of EC in Germany from the devices point of view, this work will focus mainly on platforms as drivers for EC. Where necessary, related aspects will be mentioned and described in brief.

Before turning to the different platforms for EC the perceived drivers for EC from the Andersen Consulting Research Report [AC98] are presented in Figure 4.

*Figure 4   Factors which could Enable/Accelerate EC*

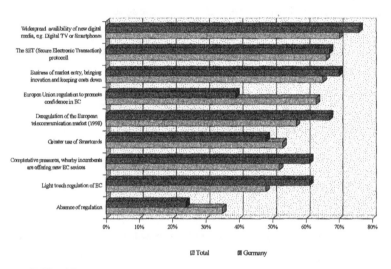

source: [AC98, p.31]

The statement 'widespread availability of new digital media', which can be seen as a synonym for new access-platforms, is assessed by 70% of the total respondents (Germany 76%) as significant. These numbers are the counterpart to the 'lack of potential customers connected barrier' (24%) in the previous chapter. Most companies see the widening of the 'installed customer-basis' through PC's and non PC devices as the most important driver for EC. The customer-supplier coherence (more customers lead to more suppliers lead to more customers) is foreseen to behave like a self emphasising circulation. For example, Forrester Research had to positively correct their EC-forecasts, as they expect a yearly 'hyper-growth' until 2003 of 70% solely in electronic retail in the US [FOR99b].

A supporting tool for EC over multiple platforms in this context are Smart-Cards, that enable authentication over multiple platforms. They are for 53% (Germany 48%) of the respondents a significant factor to enable/accelerate EC. An other important driver is the expected further deregulation of the European telecommunication market which will lead to lower telephone and internet-connection costs. This is seen by 57% of the total respondents as a potential driver. In Germany, with the highest telephone and Internet Service Provider (ISP) costs in Europe[13], the deregulation of the European telecommunication market is seen by 67% of the German respondents as a significant driver for EC.

Before turning to the next chapter Smart-Cards will be discussed in more details, as they can be implemented in almost every access device and are therefore a powerful driver of EC over multiple platforms.

**Smart-Cards**

Smart-Cards are already in widespread use in Europe, but for most users the question arises: what exactly makes a card smart?[14] Even most people are familiar with the use of credit cards as way a of cashless payment but there is a fundamental difference in functionality of Smart-Cards to other cards (e.g. credit cards). A Smart-Card is a credit-card sized plastic card embedded with an integrated circuit chip that makes it 'smart'. Two different types are to distinguish: Memory Cards and Processor Cards.
*Memory Cards:* Any plastic card is made 'smart' by including an IC chip. But the chip may simply be a memory storage device. Memory cards can hold information thousand times greater than a magnetic stripe card. Nevertheless, their functions are limited to basic applications such as phone cards or health-insurance cards.
*Processor Cards:* Smart-Cards with a full-fledged microprocessor on board can function as a processor device that offers multiple functions such as encryption, advanced security mechanism, local data processing, complex calculation and other interactive processes. Most stored-value cards integrated with identification, security and information purposes are processor cards. Only Processor-Cards are truly smart enough to offer the flexibility and multifunctionality desired in a linked-up network economy.

---

[13] The OECD estimated the 1998 off-peak Internet-access (telephone- and Internet Service Provider charge) costs for 20 hours on-line in Germany to be $74.61 vs. Finland to be $24.16 [OECD99].

[14] "Europe leads the world in the production and use of Smart-Cards, accounting for 75% of the 1.2 billion in circulation world-wide in 1997" [AC98, p.15].

These processor cards facilitate the development of EC by providing security for electronic transactions and enable micro-payments (if used as an 'electronic purse or wallet'). Smart-Cards can uniquely identify their owners through encoded certificates or digitised fingerprints, and allow encryption of messages with a users private key. Through this they provide instant and safe authorisation of payments and could provide the levels of confidence required for mass-market take-up of EC. Micro-payments can be executed through the storage function of the chip, which enables one to withdraw money from the bank account and pay in shops, restaurants or the Internet. Besides the security and payment functions of Smart-Cards, the maybe most important applications for EC over multiple platforms are its smart networking, and the integrated and customised service functions [CSWA98]. Prerequisite for this multi-functionality of Smart-Cards is an interoperable and multi-platform Application Programming Interface (API). Open standards such as Java Smart-Card API provides one of several proposed interfaces. "Java Card API in particular offers a development tool for flexible, multi-platform applications –Write Once, Run Anywhere– for devices ranging from Network Computers, Web TV, Smart-Phones and other consumer appliances" [CSWA98].

An example for the Smart Networking is the mobile telecommunication, mobile phones are gearing up to be a truly global communications network via the global GSM (Groupe Special Mobile) system. Phones come equipped with a Smart-Card slot to enable integrated services. In addition a Smart Network can also operate through a reader terminal installed at home or in offices, at a convenient store or a gas station, at an information kiosk in libraries or a phone centre at airports or even on a remote hiking trail.

Integrated and customised services for example contain Smart-Card vending systems which are used for petroleum dispensers, various vending machines and parking meters. Smart-Card based vending systems not only simplify payment processes but also enable customised services as they allow a total integration of payment, marketing and services in a networked enterprise.

After describing the potential and its use for various applications, the next chapter will describe the multiple platforms for EC in detail.

# 2 Platforms for Electronic Commerce

Platforms are devices that enable the users to execute electronic transactions. From a consumers perspective most of these devices are connected to the Internet, because it is the cheapest way of electronic connectivity to a large community. Some of the platforms described in the following do not differ in a technological manner, but from a usage perspective (e.g. mobile/stationary). Lately different platforms became more and more a serious field of research for scientists and companies, which is pushed through the trend toward specific (non PC) devices with internet connectivity and the service-centric computing approach. These special devices are designed for specific services like e-mail, web-TV, etc. They do not have the general functionality of PC's but are very convincing for their purpose.[15] The second trend leads to a more service orientated view of problem solving. More and more internet-services are used *when* needed, and less is invested in hard- and software. "Service-centric computing defines a world in which the majority of functionality and capabilities offered and supported by information technology will be operated and used as broadly available utilities" [BJ99].

The next four sub-chapters will present four platforms of EC. Not all are used with the same intensity, some are only in the early beginning to become an EC device, others are already 'well established' (if one can speak from well established in a (consumer) market, that is only 4-5 years old). Computers will be presented first, they are the most commonly used devices, next mobile phones will be analysed, for which still high growth-rates are expected in the future. Paragraph 2.3 deals with the newest platform, the Digital TV (DTV). In this paragraph it clearly shows that at this stage EC conducted via DTV is at the very early beginning in Germany. Afterwards in chapter 2.4 Public Access Points (PAPs), which are very rare in Germany (here internet-cafes are not seen as PAPs) are described, they are not as interesting from the technological aspect, but from the commodity character of the Internet.

---

[15] For example, the start-up firm AvantGO designed a software that allows people to surf the internet from their hand-held devices like the Palm Pilot or mobile phones. The WSJE expects a potentially huge market to be served with this new way of mobile access [WSJE5/99b, p.4].

## 2.1 Computer

The mainly used and most common access-platform for EC is the computer. The development of the WWW and the Browser -its standard application software - made the Computer *the* EC access-medium for the general public. In the business-to-business world EC is executed for more then 20 years by computers with EDI protocols like EFT or EDIFACT. As this study focuses more on the consumer access-platforms, EC over public networks, executed via the internet, are of premier interest.

From the server-side of EC a web-side and a database are connected to build an open information system or cyber-store. The web-side is used for advertising, searching and description of products and services. A communication interface (e.g. e-mail, user-input-mask), that enables the potential customer to order the desired products and to enter personal data of authentication and payment-details, has to be implemented. These 'web-storefronts' have to be integrated into the companies back-office (e.g. ordering, accounting) to gain the overall potential of EC.[16] If done properly: "web-storefronts integrate various functions such as physical presence as a store, sales representatives, ordering and payment functions (combined cash register, credit card reader, etc.), back-office supports and various data interchanges (for inventorying, supply ordering, etc.) " [CR99b].

Computers as platforms for EC have widespread acceptance and are powerful tools with a broad functionality. Nevertheless, as mentioned above the trend towards easy to use devices for special applications and the service-centric approach is finding more and more acceptance (by scientists and users/companies). The Computer as *the* access-medium for EC will be accompanied by various devices specialised on specific problems (e.g. communication, information, time-management, etc.). The next sections will describe in more details the new platforms which are just at the beginning of its expansion into the world of EC.

---

[16] An excellent and detailed description of relevant aspects of building web-storefronts can be found in [GP98, chapter 14].

## 2.2 Mobile Phone and other Hand-Held Devices

Through the convergence of mobile telephones and computing devices, the mobile telephones and other hand-held devices became popular channels, through which EC can be (and increasingly is) conducted. Mobile phones and other 'hand-helds' provide a gateway not only to products and services made available by particular mobile phone companies, but also to products and services available on the internet. Phones operating to the GSM (Groupe Special Mobile) digital standard have the further advantage of operating in every European country. In addition they typically have an in-built Smart-Card for identification and security purpose, so that products and services bought can be charged to the mobile phone bills.

The new mobile internet connectivity is possible through the General Packet Radio Services (GPRS) that enables the devices to transact in a packet orientated manner (TCP/IP). It expands the GSM standard which is connection orientated. GPRS expands the GSM by package ability through a dynamic time-slot generation mechanism that enables transmission rates of 115 kilobytes [CZ99b, p.14]. Another standard is HSCSD (High-speed Circuit Switched Data) that supports permanent high bandwidth for applications like videoconferencing. Companies like Nokia, 3Com or Microsoft are working with high-pressure on applications that support mobile data-exchange over devices like pager, hand-devices, mobile phones or laptops.[17] Major companies in the IT-business compete to set standards for this future market. Gartner Research writes: "the company [Microsoft] has made several significant moves designed ostensibly to make it a mainstream player in the wireless data arena" [GAR99]. 70 major players (e.g. Unwired Planet, Ericsson, Motorola) formed the WAP-Forum (Wireless Application Protocol) in 1997 to develop a uniform standard of mobile web-surfing. The potential in this area of EC platforms/accesses can be estimated by powerful alli-

---

[17] Microsoft and British Telecom announced a joint venture in February 1999 that promotes the wireless access on web-based services like e-mail, scheduling or web-pages through non computer devices with Microsoft's CE operating system [WSJE99c, p.14].

33

ances created in the past. These alliances offer a widespread range of services from networks over browsers to devices that offer an all in one service to the user.[18]

*German Mobile Phone Market*

In the beginning of 1999 in Germany approx. 14.5 million persons had a mobile phone contract [DTEL99,D2P99,VIA99,EPLU99].[19] Presently in Germany two different GSM systems are in use, the GSM 900 from D1 and D2 Privat and the GSM 1800 from E Plus and E2.

## 2.3 Digital TV

The broad penetration and acceptance of analogue TV led to the Digital TV (DTV) approach as a new interactive communication device for various multi-media applications. Digital TV combines the convenience and acceptance of TV and the widespread functionality of the internet or other information-networks. Digital signals are received via satellite, cable, broad-band, or A/C power receivers and are converted through set-top-boxes (or in-built receivers) to TV-signals. User-interfaces like keyboards, remote-controls or voice-converters enable the interaction with the device.

The importance of Digital TV as an EC platform arises from its extended functionality, which are in particular [DVB99a]:

- more channels through standard definition Digital TV (SDTV) and better images through high definition TV (HDTV);

- enhanced services through convergence of TV and Computer (from simple interactive quiz shows, to internet over the air, and mix of television and web-type content);[20]

---

[18] Motorola, Nextel and Netscape will offer a internet service for mobile users. Nextel offers the network, Netscape the portal and Motorola the devices with in-built modem and browser from UP [CZ99a, p.7].

[19] These number spreads out between the different mobile telephone companies as follows: D2 Privat 6.5 million in 3/99, Deutsche Telekom 5.5 million (D1) and 0.37 million (C-Net) in 1/99, E Plus 2 million in 1/99 and E2 0.1 million in 4/99.

[20] Microsoft's WebTV offers an integration of TV and internet, it has 400,000 subscribers in the US [ECM99, p.XI].

- television (and other devices) on the move: with DTV (in contrary to analogue TV) the possibility has opened up in providing crystal clear television, to sets in mobile use.

Today most of the television equipment in production is already digital. The problem is the lack in digital consumer end-devices. Early attempts of Digital TV stand out of a variety of standards, each set by different companies. The struggle for dominance in the future market of Digital TV is a serious barrier to the adoption of this new technology. Customers fear the potential dependence to a single broadcaster or equipment manufacturer. In Germany, the first broadcast station offering Digital TV was the Pay TV station DF1, which only can be received via Nokia's dbox (set-top-box). However, the latter is struggling to broaden the subscriber-bases (of 180,000 in October 1998) since it launched its program in 1997 [BR98]. The solution are open platform standards which can receive various digital applications and are open for new services. In Germany the F.U.N. (Free Universe Network), formed by media and technology companies, was established in February 1999 to promote and develop the free DTV in Germany. Its recommendations are orientated at the DVB (Digital Video Broadcasting) definitions of Common Interfaces (CI) which are already standard (by law) in most European countries, and can be seen in Figure 5 on the next page.[21]

---

[21] The Digital Video Broadcasting Project (DVB) includes over 220 well known organisations in more than 30 countries world-wide. An overview of the recommended standards can be found in [DVB99a].

*Figure 5 Countries Accepting the DVB Standards*

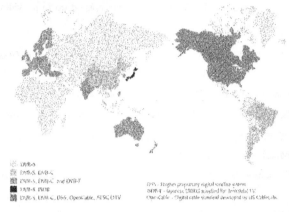

source: [DVB99b]

F.U.N.'s aim is to guarantee competition, variety and unhindered access to the market place for potential participants. This should be guaranteed through a definition of a universal, open platform, which is the base for various digital applications. The new Multimedia Home Platform (MHP) is based on the virtual machine which is able to execute Java and HTML/XML programs [BR98]. The central issues of the F.U.N. platform-approach are [FUN99]:

- the basic DVB-Standards of transmission, video- and audio-encoding and service-information;

- the Application Programming Interface (API);

- the DVB-Common Interface.

The F.U.N. 'universal digital decoder' operates on an open operating system called Open TV EN which is able to work on Java and HTML, and consists of a published API (Application Programming Interface). These decoders are equipped with 2 PCMCIA Common Interfaces (like a computer) which serve as universal interfaces that can be connected to the PC, the Internet, the telephone etc..

The general structure of this open platform is displayed in Figure 6. Every F.U.N. member has to follow mandatory features that guarantee the inter-operationality of several devices.

*Figure 6 F.U.N. Platformtechnology*

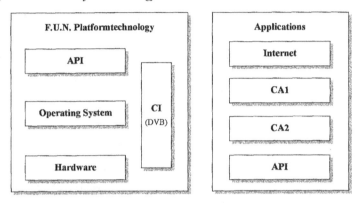

source: [FUN99]

This is possible through the publishing of API's, that follow the DVB Common Interface (CI) definitions. Following these guidelines, various Conditional Access (CA) Systems, Internet and other applications become possible.

In the US, open platforms for Digital TV through Common Interfaces (PCMCIA) are legally stipulated from the FCC (Federal Communication Commission) by the year 2001, to counteract the monopolisation.[22] In the following empirical examinations it will not be distinguished between open and closed Digital TV. Most of the DTV in Germany and Europe is still operated in a closed (mostly Pay TV) system. Nevertheless, these systems offer enhanced services like home-shopping or video-on-demand and therefore count to the EC platforms by definition of this work.

---

[22] The FCC is a US standardisation authority which discharges recommendations standards in the communication field [FCC99].

For the description of the German Digital TV market, the market-study from Galaxis, a manufacturer of digital and analogue satellite technology, will be discussed below [GAL98].

At the end of 1998 37.4 million households were counted in Germany. From these households 37.2% received their TV program via satellite (analogue or digital), 44.1% via channel and 16.7% terrestrial. Only 2.0% had no TV. In 1998 the quota of digital satellite receivers amounted only 23% of the total receivers in use. This apportionment is expected to increase to 70% in 2004, which corresponds to 1.5 million pieces to be sold in this year. 397 TV Programs where receivable in 1998 digital via satellite receivers (Astra and Eutelsat) in Germany.

Next Public Access Points (PAP) and Vending Machines are presented. Vending Machines for EC are still in the early stage and provide the basic application for the trend toward a cash-less society (internet cafes are not in this category, they are covered in the computer-platform section).

## 2.4 Public Access Points and Vending Machines

Today, most of the existing Public Access Points (PAP) or Vending Machines work on credit or telephone cards. These cards are more or less only the vehicle of a cash-less payment system. In the future these PAP's or Vending Machines will work with Smart-Cards and will be embedded into a smart-networking-system [CSWA98]. The difference is that in a Smart Network the devices (e.g. public terminals) will be able to offer personalised contents, depending on the users demand.[23] Schlumberger, the largest Smart-Card seller illustrates the vision of a networked world where Smart-Card based services and products inhabit the every day live. Schlumberger's Smart Village include: GSM payphones and mobile telecommunication, private site smart pay phones, smart ticket vending machines at transit terminals, smart pay and display units at parking lots, smart fuel dispenser at gas stations, contactless, remote and pre-

---

[23] The Smart-Card works like a platform for cookies to take away.

paid card terminals in retail locations, smart health care management and network access based on secured, personalised Smart-Cards [SLB99].

This vision is of cause driven by commercial interest of Schlumberger as a card seller, but the convenience and widespread acceptance in the use of cards as an authentication and payment medium makes Smart-Cards to a potential enabler of smart networking.

Theses personalised PAP's in a Smart Network will have to compete with the new hand-devices described in chapter 2.2. The successes will mainly depend on two aspects: the affordability of hand-devices (costs) and the powerfulness of the applications running on the different devices (e.g. how powerful will the micro-browsers in hand-helds be?) to exchange data.

Nevertheless, PAP's and Vending-Machines will change the way people communicate (in some part). Electronic mailing, info-on-demand, etc. will become natural element in the all-day live of the general public. PAP's will also promote the development to net-centric computing, where less is invested in hardware and more is paid for content-use.

*German Public Access Point and Vending Machines Market*

Within the described access platforms, PAP's and Vending Machines are the less used access platforms in Germany. If in use, they only function as pilots in an EC project of various suppliers. In chapter 4, one PAP platform which is tested since last winter by Deutsche Telekom in Germany will be described. Unfortunately during this work no concise figures were available about its penetration in Germany (even Deutsche Telekom did not know how many PAPs they operate, as different small independent projects are running at the same time).

# 3 Electronic Commerce in Germany

The following section describes the use of EC and the underlying infrastructure in Germany compared to Europe, US or the World. The data is based on research found in the literature and in two surveys undertaken in Berlin from May to July 1999. One survey was focused on company experts and was carried out via e-mail or interviews. The second survey was a general questionnaire focused on the public use of the Internet, which was done in Berlin via personal interviews (random selection), e-mails and a temporary web page.

## 3.1 Electronic Commerce Volume in Germany

First of all, to get an impression of the economic size of EC, its current market volume and the forecasts for Germany and Europe are presented in Figure 7. Roland Berger estimates an EC sales volume in Germany of 27.8 billion DM in 2001, up 6,850 % from its actual 0.4 billion DM in 1998.

*Figure 7  Estimated Internet Sales in Germany and Europe*

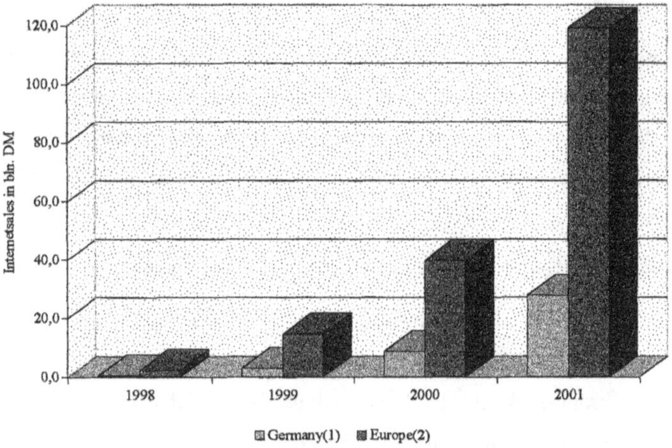

source: (1) [RB99]; (2) [FOR98]

This impressive growth is accompanied by Forrester's forecast for Europe as a whole, which is estimated to rise around 5,305 % to 118.9 billion DM in 2001 from its actual 2.2 billion in 1998. The expected growth rates reflect the companies high expectations in EC, which was presented in chapter 1.5.

Nevertheless, these figures should only give an impression of the expected growthrates, they are very volatile depending on which source is being used. This arises from the general problem of appropriate internet measurement methods and the different basis on which these forecasts are based.[24] Most of these forecasts are generated through surveys undertaken by consulting companies or market research institutes, which are forced to present 'concise' figures.

As described in chapter 1.1.2, EC can be executed between different economic entities. The most important from the economic perspective are consumers and companies. Internet sales can be partitioned between Business to Business (BB) and Business to Consumer (BC). In 1997, 65% of the internet-sales were taken out between companies (BB) and 35% between companies and consumers (BC) (see Figure 8).

*Figure 8  Partitioning of Internet Sales in Germany (1997)*

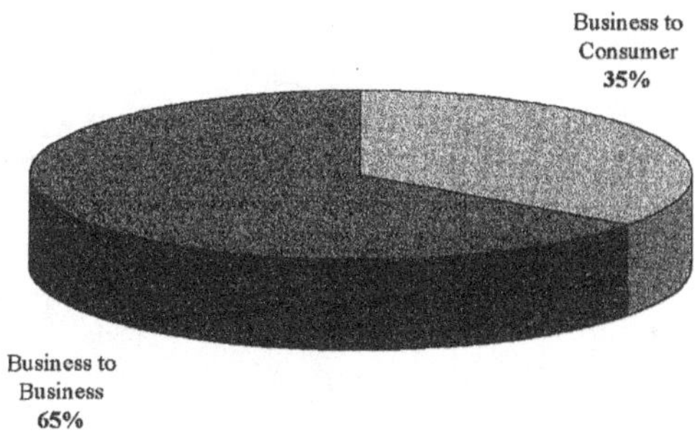

Source: [ECO97]

Most of the Business to Business transactions were carried out via EDI, the best established EC medium (see chapter 1.3). The proportion of the Internet sales (BB/BC) are relative stable as both parts are expected to grow vastly. Interesting is the relative high proportion of BC Internet sales measured by ECO [ECO97]. However, EC in Germany (1997) was at an early stage.

---

[24] A lot of data found in the Internet is published without a solid definition of the data-gathering method or only abstracts of surveys are presented.

## 3.2 Electronic Commerce Infrastructure in Germany

The first approach to estimate the growth of EC or the Internet in general is the counting of internet-hosts (computers connected to the Internet), which has been undertaken since the beginning of the Internet. Figure 9 presents this data for the years 1993 to 1998 for Germany, Europe and the World.

*Figure 9   Development of Internet-Hosts in Germany, Europe and the World*

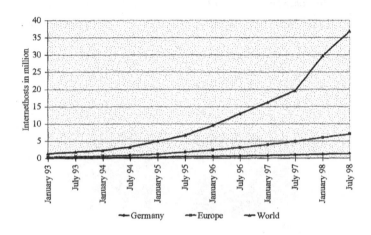

source: [CC99]

This data shows, that compared to the growth of the numbers of internet-hosts in Europe as a whole and in the World, the German growth is relative slow (see Figure 9). The world-wide numbers of internet-hosts grew from 1.3 million in 1993 to 36.7 million in 1998. This strong annual average growth of 187% (geometric mean) is mostly caused through the exploding growth in the US, where the Internet was adopted by the public much earlier than in Europe. The relative numbers (host per user), data is expected to converge in the long run because the growth in Europe is catching up and the growth in US is slowing down. Furthermore, Europe is quite divergent in the relative numbers of hosts. For example, Finland was at the top of relative numbers of internet hosts with 89 hosts per 1,000 inhabitants, compared to Germany with only 17 hosts per 1,000 inhabitants in 1998 [ETO99a].[25]

A detailed analysis of these figures would go beyond the intention of this work, although the comparison yields to a variety of interesting results about the competitiveness of 'well developed' countries like Germany.

Besides the measurement of quantitative data like internet-hosts, it is important to look at qualitative aspects as well. Especially for EC applications it is important that the underlying infrastructure is able to handle huge data within short time. This is guaranteed through redundant servers and high bandwidth. High bandwidth enables applications like video-on-demand, tele-medicine, etc. Important is the separation between backbone-technology and access-bandwidth, because for the further development of EC high data-streams into the households, will have to be handled, to make shopping or other services more convenient. Examples for such access-lines with high bandwidth are ISDN (Integrated Services Digital Network) or ADSL (Asymmetrical Digital Subscriber Line).

In Germany the penetration of these high-bandwidth lines is on a relatively high level. At the end of 1998 in Germany 10.1 million ISDN lines were in use [DTEL98, p37]. The leading position in the field of ISDN lines can be estimated by comparing the ISDN lines per 1000 main lines. In 1997, in Germany 39 out of 1,000 lines were ISDN lines. In France for example there were only 16 and in Denmark there were only 9 out of 1,000 lines ISDN [ETO99b]. Furthermore, Deutsche Telekom announced the extension of ADSL lines into 33 urban centres [TEL99, p.42]. Also the backbone technology for the data transfer has been improved during the last years considerably. Germany has a full-coverage ATM (Asynchronous Transfer Mode) telephone-net with 42 admission knots [TEL99, p.42].

After describing the development of the technological infrastructure of the Internet, next sales and user demographics using this infrastructure will be discussed in detail.

---

[25] A good overview of relative numbers concerning Internet and EC data is held by the EU and the OECD; for example [ETO99a] and [OECD98].

The empirical data is based on various examinations of different market-researches or consulting companies.

## 3.3 Internet-Use in Germany

### 3.3.1 Access

In the business section of EC the growth of users and hosts are relatively strong correlated as most companies run their own internet-servers (hosts). In the consumer section both figures are not correlated, as most users access the Internet via an Internet Service Provider (ISP) or Online Service, where many users share a few hosts. This fact is presented in Figure 10, where the number of private users and companies connected to the Internet in Germany are presented. The difference between hosts and users can be seen in Figure 10 (e.g. for the year 1998), where hosts and users are compared. In 1998 in Germany 7.3 million users where counted by Roland Berger [RB99]. At the same time in Germany 1.31 million Internet hosts existed. Furthermore Figure 10 shows that at the present more individuals are connected to the Internet privately than via companies. However, business-connections are expected to catch up and exceed the number of private connections in 2001.

*Figure 10   Germans Connected to the Internet*

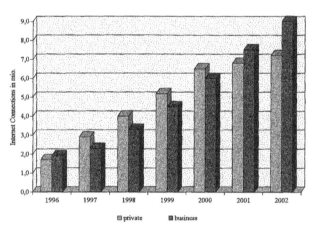

source: [RB99]

More interesting than the absolute figures are 'relative numbers' which are comparable between countries. This is done in Figure 11, where the number of Internet-users per inhabitant in Germany and USA are compared.

*Figure 11 Internet-User per Inhabitant (Penetration) in Germany and the US*

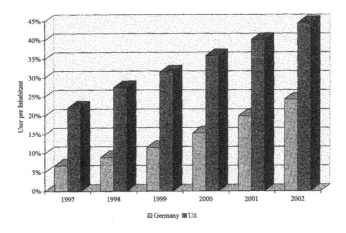

source: [ECIN99], [ETO99a]                              (Inhabitants 1997-2002 constant)

The figure shows the large gap in the penetration of the Internet between the US and Germany. In the US the adoption by the broad mass is much further than in Germany. In the year 2002 every second inhabitant in the US is expected to be an internet-user in some way or another. A fact that shows that the Internet is becoming an everyday commodity good like the TV or the telephone. Although in Germany the Internet is far away from being an all day commodity good, as only less than 10% were users in 1998, the figures are no reason for resigning. Notwithstanding the low adoption-rate by the broad mass in Germany at present, the growth-rates are expected to increase and the gap is expected to become smaller in the long run. The discussed figures of German internet-users can not be generalised for Europe as a whole, as in Europe the data is very divergent (see Appendix C). For example, in August 1998 Finland had a penetration of 27.9%, where as in Greece it was only 1% [FOC99]. Generally the Nordic countries in Europe have a much higher penetration of users than the rest of Europe.

In the following text, the users' demographics and their preferences are discussed for Germany. For this, a study undertaken by the GfK (Gesellschaft für Konsumforschung), a market-researcher in Germany, is presented below [GFK99]. The *GfK Online Monitor* is undertaken every half-year in spring and autumn. For this 3$^{rd}$ study 5,662 people in telephone-households between the ages of 14-59 years were interviewed. The sample is corresponding to 44.3 million or approx. 50% of the German population.

Figure 12 shows that the user-base grew about 40% compared to the last survey 6 months ago. 8.4 million people between the ages of 14 and 59 years , which is 19% of the sample, used the Internet occasionally. The out-of-home use is still dominating, 5.4 million people accessed the Internet from places outside their households. Contrasting to this, 4.9 million used online-media from their homes.

*Figure 12  Internet-Access in Germany*

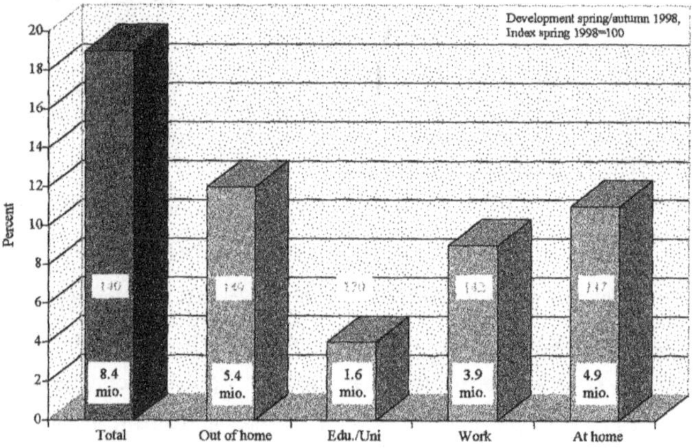

source: [GFK99]

The way how people access the web differs between Germany and the US, which is characteristic for the commodity character of the Internet in the different countries. In the US 78% of the users accessed the web on a daily basis from home. Almost a third of the respondents never accessed the Web from work [GVU98, p.4]. Furthermore, GVU found that the majority of the respondents (71.5%) have never accessed the web from a public terminal. For Germany this kind of data was not available, but 6%

of the German internet-users answered, that they access the web from Internet Cafes [W3B99]. In this context it has to be mentioned that the comparison of the different surveys has to be done very carefully, as the data-bases and the ways of data-gathering differ significantly. The GfK survey is a representative survey, interviewing users and non-users, where as the two other surveys (W3B and GVU) are not representative. The last two surveys interviewed only users, as the questionnaire were only available on the Internet. Therefore, both methods offer preferences of users, but a direct comparison is difficult and has to be done carefully.

## 3.3.2 User Demographics

Figure 13 to Figure 15 present the users demographic characteristics. These figures show that the web is still mostly used by young, male and relative good trained persons. But these figures are changing towards the average structure of the analysed country. In Germany 69% of the users were males, which is relatively equal to the US, there were 66.7% were males [GVU99] (see Figure 13).

*Figure 13  Gender of German Internet-Users*

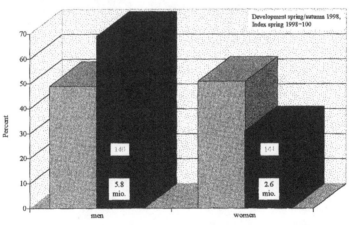

□ Total population 14-59 years ■ 3rd survey user

source: [GFK99]

For the age-structure the data is relatively similar to the average population structure in the middle range (30-49 years). For the 14-19 years and the 40-59 years sections the user structure differs from the average population structure (see Figure 14). The adoption of the Internet in the over 50 years section developed relatively hesitant. For the US, GVU found an average age of 37.6 years for the internet-user, where as the corresponding average age of the German internet-user was 30.9 years [GVU99]. Again this can be explained by the adoption progress of the Internet.

*Figure 14 Age of German Internet-Users*

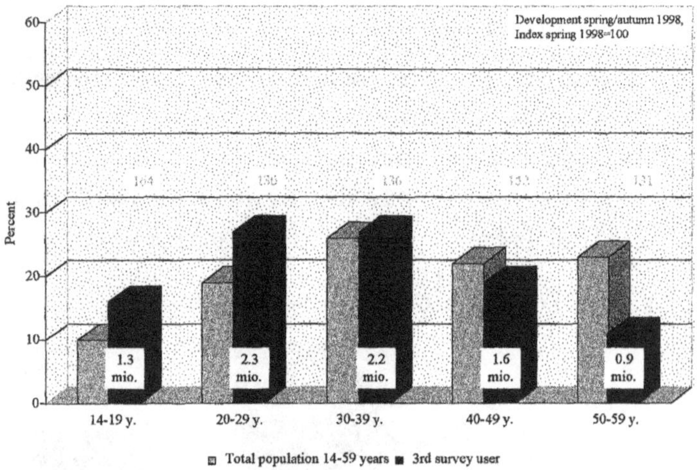

source: [GFK99]

For the qualification level, Figure 15 shows that in Germany a demographic gap between the average population structure and the internet-user structure is still existing.
The web is used in excess in the University and Collage Broad Exam sections, compared to their sizes in the population. The Junior High-School section is using the web
sub-proportional relative to its size, but has the largest growth-rates. These growth-
rates show that an adjustment towards the average population demographics is taking
place.

*Figure 15  Qualification of German Internet-Users*

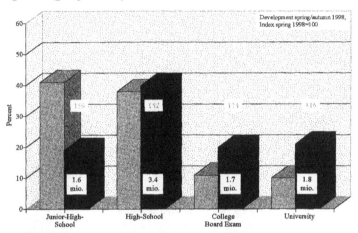

source: [GFK99]

After describing the infrastructure, the sales-volume and the user-demographics, the
EC content is presented next, to give answers to the questions: '*what* are people buying via the Web and *why* are they buying certain things and others not'.

### 3.3.3 Content

First of all Figure 16 shows that only 42% of the German internet-users have EC experience because they already bought products or services on the Web. 57.3% of the users have never bought anything via the internet (see Figure 16). However, these numbers are expected to change in the future. If asked for their purchase intention during the next 6 month, only 21% of the respondents answered that they are not planing to buy anything, 37% answered yes and 42% maybe (see Figure 16). Therefore, even in Germany the Internet is recognised by more and more users as an important sales-medium.

*Figure 16 Buying Experience vs. Intention to Buy via Internet*

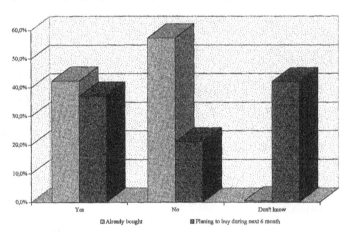

**source:** [W3B99]

Not all products and services are equally well suited for online selling. In the products section best selling products were goods that are standardised sold in large numbers and well known from offline selling.

These are for example CDs, books and clothing, which sales in the past grew rapidly (see Figure 17). Software and household products are still sold in large numbers but less then in the last GfK survey.

*Figure 17  Best-Selling Products via Internet*

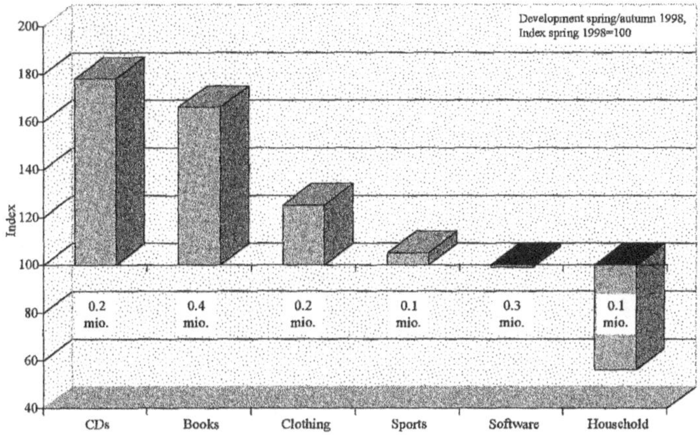

Another section of online-trading with even stronger growth-rates during the past 6 months are services which were used by 33% or 2.8 million of the users. During spring 1998 they were only used by 1.8 million [GFK99]. Booking of train-/flight-journeys, as well as travel- and hotel-bookings were the most used services (see Figure 18 next page).

They had enormous increases during the last 6 months (flight-bookings grew over 300%). As with the online selling of products the standardisation of services are the most powerful aspect of the demand for online-services. Flight and hotel prices are easily comparable and the performance are standardised (e.g. flight Berlin-New York). Furthermore home-banking, other bank-services and insurance-services were used by less people online then in the last survey. Interesting is that the banks were the pioneers in the EC consumer section with their home-banking services.

*Figure 18  Best-Selling Services via Internet*

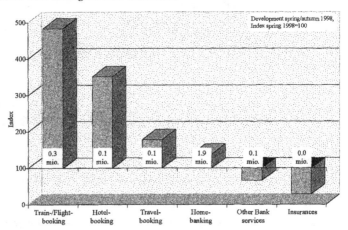

source: [GFK99]

As described in chapter 1.3 the main power underlying EC is the reduction of transaction costs. How this theoretical framework works in practice can be seen by the fact that for standardised products and services, the Internet helps to reduce search and information costs (which are part of the transaction costs). Therefore, these products and services are the best-selling ones which had such impressive increase in the past 6 months.

Besides the theoretical explanation of the Internet as a sales medium, people were asked to give their statement why they prefer the Internet for the shopping of selected products and services (see Figure 19).

*Figure 19  Why do People Shop via the Internet?*

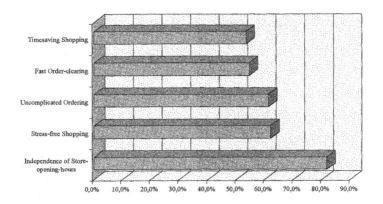

81.5% of the respondents answered that they prefer the web for shopping because of its independence from store-opening hours, which unfortunately are in Germany still very restricted. Furthermore, 61% of the respondents named the uncomplicated ordering and the stress-free shopping as an advantage of online-shopping. Interesting is that the time-saving aspect of online-shopping and the fast order-clearing is only seen by approx. 50% of the respondents as a reason to shop the Internet. This is a note for the existing problem to handle the information flood of the Internet, which shows the need for tools like smart agents, which handle this problem.

After describing the found data in the literature, in the following two surveys undertaken during May and July 1999 are presented. The aim of these studies were to get additional platform-specific information. Furthermore, they can be seen as a testing of special aspects also handled in the discussed surveys above.

## 3.4 Expert Questionnaire

Below the evaluation of the expert questionnaire (see Appendix A) is presented and its main results discussed briefly. The Interviews were undertaken during the 16th and 17th of May at the Internet World (Fair) in Berlin and via e-mailing to different IT and Management representatives of companies involved in EC. Its aim was the information gathering about perceived potentials and barriers of EC. Furthermore various forecasts of the growth-potentials for the different platforms discussed in Chapter 2 should be compared.[26] 18 respondents from the total 36 persons (=N) interviewed answered question 5 (growth forecasts of EC platforms) of the questionnaire complete or in parts (data is presented in Appendix A). The questionnaire is supported in most cases by the two surveys of Andersen Consulting and KPMG, discussed in chapter 1.5.

56% of the respondents belonged to the Management/Marketing division, 17% to the IT division and 28% to others (e.g. sales). The selection procedure was done by the specific cluster sample rule. The idea was to get a balanced mixture of the respondents belonging to the management division (approx. 50%) and other divisions (IT o.a.). 67% of the companies examined, had already implemented EC in some way. From the companies which had not implemented EC so far (33%), 50% are planing to implement EC during the next 6 months (17% later and 33% are not planing an implementation).

After describing the sample characteristics, the more interesting questions of the respondents assessments of the potentials and barriers of EC and the forecasts for the different platforms will be discussed next.

**Potentials of EC**

The questions of EC´s potential to improve business transactions (Q.1.1) and workflow (Q.1.2) were answered by 83% of the total respondents, with strong or very

---

[26] Unfortunately only a few respondents passed a valuation for the growth of the different platforms on; either because people interviewed did not know exact figures or because companies did not want to offer their forecasts, as they are seen as company confidentially. Therefore this work presents the forecasts of some companies, statistical analyses is not undertaken as the data would not be representative.

strong (see Figure 20 next page). The same is valid for its potential to improve product presentation/information (Q.1.3) which were also seen by 83% of the respondents as strong or very strong (see Figure 20). These three topics of EC were the main drivers discussed in chapter 1.5.2. Question 1.1 and 1.2 deals with the cost reducing aspects of EC, 1.3 the revenue increasing factor. Both are recognised as highly relevant for the future. Furthermore, EC is seen as a powerful sales medium (Q.1.4) as 72% of the respondents assess its potential as strong or very strong (see Figure 20). Although seen by most of the respondents as a strong sales-medium, question 1.4 is answered more divergent then the 3 questions before (28% do not agree). The same is valid for the question of EC´s potential to optimise payment transactions (Q.1.5). Here only 61% agreed strong or very strong that EC has strong potential (see Figure 20). 22% - more than in any other question before - see only poor or very poor optimisation potentials in payment transactions through EC. Question 1.5 has therefore the highest variance of 48%[27]. The divergence of the last two questions are explicable by the still existing (perceived) threats of insecure payment methods.

*Figure 20  Assessment of EC Potentials*

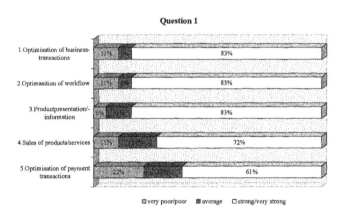

**Question 1**

| | | |
|---|---|---|
| 1.Optimisation of business-transactions | 11% | 83% |
| 2.Optimasition of workflow | 11% | 83% |
| 3.Productpresentation/-information | 6% | 83% |
| 4.Sales of products/services | 11% | 72% |
| 5.Optimisation of payment transactions | 22% | 61% |

▨ very poor/poor    ▦ average    ☐ strong/very strong

---

[27] Variance in proportion to the span width of the scale (5).

55

The same conclusions were drawn from the KPMG and Andersen Consulting studies in chapter 1.5. Therefore, the results of this expert questionnaire are supported by their much larger data basis.

**Barriers of EC**

The questions concerning the barriers of EC were partially similar to the aspects treated in the KPMG and Andersen Consulting surveys in chapter 1.5.1. The respondents were asked to rate the questions 6.1 to 6.6 (from strong no to strong yes). The results are much more divergent then the data presented above. An explanation could be that the barriers are more technical orientated than the potentials (as everyone has ideas about the potentials of EC in general) and therefore the answers are highly correlated to the respondents IT know-how.

78% of the respondents see the insecure payment procedures as a strong barrier, they answered question 6.1 with yes or strong yes (see Figure 21). The lack of authentication of business-partners were only seen by 44% as a strong or very strong barrier (Q.6.2), the same percentage is valid for the complexity of handling EC devices (Q.6.3) (see Figure 21).

*Figure 21 Assessment of EC Barriers*

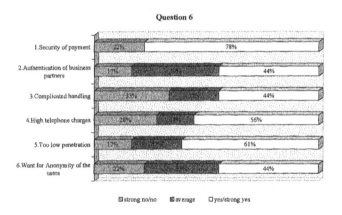

Furthermore, the respondents were asked if they see a barrier in high (telephone) connection prices (Q.6.4). Question 6.4 is the most contrary answered amongst the one of barrier questions concerning the variance (50.8%). This is explicable by the fact that on the one hand high connection prices are seen as a potential barrier, but on the other hand prices are expected to decrease. Next the respondents were asked to rate if the low penetration of EC/internet-access is a barrier (Q.6.5). This question was answered by 61% with yes or strong yes, which reflects the critical-mass-aspect of EC. Last the respondents were asked if they see the desire for anonymity of the users as a barrier of EC (Q.6.5). Here only 44% answered with yes or strong yes, 22% did not agree (see Figure 21).

As argued above in the potentials of EC conclusion, this first source data analysis of the barriers of EC is mostly supported by the surveys from KPMG and Andersen Consulting presented in chapter 1.5.1.

Last, the assessments of the development of different access platforms and the forecasts of the growth potential given by selected companies (Microsoft, GfK, Novalabs) involved in EC are presented.

**Assessment of EC platforms**

In Question 3.1 to 3.5 of the expert questionnaire the respondents were asked to give their personal assessments of different access platforms for the future (agree/not agree). The results are presented in Figure 22 (next page). As can be seen, all the new access media are estimated in such a manner, to be used even stronger in the future. Mobile phones are estimated to play a major role in the future by 72% (Q.3.1), Digital TV by 78% (Q.3.2) and Public Access Points by 72% (Q.3.3). Furthermore, the respondents were asked to rate whether people would buy more via Internet if the handling would be easier (Q.3.4). Here only 61% agreed, which indicates that experts see potential to improve the way of access to the Internet. Last, the respondents were asked if they think the interactive household will soon be reality (Q.3.5). Question 3.5 is the most divergent answered question in this section, as only 50% answered this question with yes. The subject of pervasive computing (here understood as a technology enabling the interactive household) is amongst the presented questions the most IT-specific question. Therefore, even IT experts (from other fields) are not quite sure about current technical solutions and the users interests. These specifics lead to an overall sceptical assessment of the pervasive computing segment.

*Figure 22  Assessment of Different EC Topics*

Percentage agreeing that...

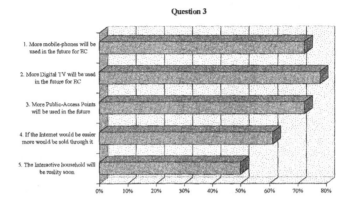

**Question 3**

1. More mobile-phones will be used in the future for EC

2. More Digital TV will be used in the future for EC

3. More Public-Access Points will be used in the future

4. If the Internet would be easier more would be sold through it

5. The Interactive household will be reality soon

0%   10%   20%   30%   40%   50%   60%   70%   80%

**Microsoft's, GfK's and Novalabs' forecasts of EC platform growth**

As mentioned in the beginning of this chapter, only a few forecasts of the development of EC platforms from selected companies are presented (Microsoft, GfK and Novalabs). An aggregation of the results will be refrained because the small database of answers for question 5 would not lead to representative conclusions.

*Growth-Rate of PC's (Q.5.1)*

Microsoft estimates a growth of PC´s from the end of 1999 to 2003 of 100% (from 15 million to 30 million) a penetration of approx. 35%. GfK predicts PCs to increase from 15 million at the end of 1999 to 25 million, and in the year 2003, a growth of 67% is expected. The same growth-rate is estimated by Novalabs, but they start from 12 million at the end of 1999 going up to 20 million in the year 2003 (see Figure 23 next page).

*Growth-Rate of Households with Internet-Access (Q.5.2)*

For the development of internet-accesses in households Microsoft and GfK estimate the same growth-rate of 300% (5 million at end of 1999 to 20 million in 2003). Compared to this, Novalabs forecasts differ extremely from the other two, as they only see a growth-rate of 100% (from 8 million to 16 million) (see Figure 23). This large gap

59

shows the widespread assessment differences caused by measurement problems (mentioned in the beginning of this work) and indicates estimation differences of the adoption speed of the Internet.

*Figure 23   Growth of EC Platforms in Germany 1999-2003*

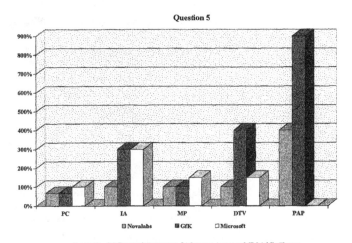

**Legend:**   PC Personal Computers, IA Internet Accesses, MP Mobile Phones,
DTV Digital TV, PAP Public Access Points

*Growth-Rates of Mobile Phones (Q.5.3)*

The growth-rates of mobile phones are not expected to be as large as in the Internet-access section. But starting from a much larger basis of 20 million at the end of 1999 the absolute numbers are very impressive. As mentioned in chapter 2.2, at the beginning of 1999 in Germany approx. 14.5 million people had a mobile phone contract. Therefore, mobile phones are expected to grow 38% within 1999 and furthermore a growth-rate of 150% (Novalabs only 100%), which results in 50 million (40 million) in the year 2003, is expected (see Figure 23). This will be a penetration of over 50% of the German population, a number that was reached by the Scandinavians in 1998. These results go hand in hand with Andersen Consulting's analysis of past PC and mobile phone growth-rate comparisons. They estimated a growth-rate of PCs from 1996 to 1997 of only 14% whereas it was 57% for mobile phones [AC98, p.14].

*Growth-Rates of Digital TV (Q.5.4)*

The results from question 5.4 are very contrary, Microsoft for example estimates a growth of 150% for Digital TVs (from 2 million 1999 to 5 million 2003), whereas GfK forecasts an enormous growth of 400% (from 3 million 1999 to 15 million 2003) (see Figure 23). This divergence is caused mainly because Digital TV in Germany is still in the early beginning and the expected 'hyper-growth' of adoption has not taken place so far (and its start is unsure at the present). From the presented platforms for EC, Digital TV is the one with the most distinctive differences for consumers to existing use of EC devices (Computer, PAP). The reason for this is that in the last 50 years TV worked only one-way. Different devices to handle the information gathering via DTV were tested in the past (keyboard, voice-recognition, remote-control, etc.). Although the technological solutions are already available, consumer adoption is still lagging behind.

*Growth-Rates of Public-Access Points (PAPs) (Q.5.5)*

PAPs are not interesting from the technological view, as they are mostly only PCs at public places (although possibly operating with Smart-Cards in the future). Like with Digital TV, GfK is much more optimistic about the growth-rates then Microsoft or Novalabs. Because of the enormous differences of the estimations in this section (GfK 1000%, Microsoft no growth), the reality has to be somewhere in-between. Reliable forecasts are therefore difficult to state and existing results have to be read with scepticism.

After analysing the company expert's assessments of the future development of EC and its access platforms, a general questionnaire undertaken from May to July (1999) in Berlin will be presented in the following.

## 3.5 General Questionnaire

This questionnaire (see Appendix B) was undertaken throughout the 3 participating countries, covered by the three students of this research project. The results will at the end of the project, be combined to a European perspective of the assessment of the Internet and its functionality as a sales-medium via various platforms. This survey was undertaken via e-mailing, a web-page[28] and personal interviews. Its aim was to get a picture of the internet-experience and the assessment of different EC platforms of ordinary, German respondents. 82 (=N) respondents gave their feedback, 25 via e-mail, 16 via the web page and 41 in personal interviews (data is presented in Appendix B). Although an effort was made to obtain an average mixture of internet-users and non-users, the results show that the sample converges strongly towards the internet-users, as 72% of the respondents had internet-access, either at home or at work (Q.1). In contrast to this, GfK found that only 19% of the households had internet-access (see chapter 3.3.1). Therefore the following conclusions have to be seen in respect to the sample-demographics. Although a generalisation for the German population is not recommended (in addition the sample-size would be much to small), the results, however, give an interesting insights of the attitudes of the respondents towards the examined platforms of EC.

If asked whether products or services were bought via the Internet or not, 37% answered with yes (Q.2). If splitting the question between respondents who answered the questionnaire electronically (e-mail/web-page) or in a personal interview, then the result looks slightly different. 48% of the e-mail respondents and 63% of the web-page respondents have already bought goods or services via the Internet, whereas only 20% of the respondents did so from the personal interviews. Moreover, if looking at the aspect 'internet-access' vs. 'no internet-access', then the results from question 2 are very similar to the one found by W3B (see Figure 16). 44% of the respondents with internet-access have already bought goods or services via the Internet, and only 17% of respondents did so without internet-access. Interesting is that these 17% of the respondents have bought without an own internet-access at home or at work, which indicates that a personal access-device is not mandatorily necessary for online-buying - a strong pro for PAPs.

In question 3, respondents were asked to state their assessment to various internet-related topics. The statement 'The Internet is complicated and shopping over the Internet is even more complicated' (Q.3.a), this was answered by only 27% positively,

---

[28] The web page was running from the 1 June to 25 July 1999 within the computer science laboratory of the institute of information systems at the Humboldt University zu Berlin.

which shows that the Internet is seen by most of the respondents as a commodity product. This result can be further analysed: 25% of the 'internet-access respondents' and 30% of the 'no internet-access respondents' agreed to this question. The question 3.b 'The interactive household will be reality in 5 years' was suspiciously answered by 46% with yes, which seems to be inexplicable in connection with question 3.c 'Being able to order goods and services sitting in the sofa is enough reason to buy a Digital TV-set' which was only answered by 26% of the respondents with yes.[29] This gap can again be explained if the two groups are divided, as 48% of the 'no access-respondents' agreed to this question, which indicates that not the online-shopping by itself but the 'complicated' handling of a computer is seen as a problem. The next question (Q.3.d) asked whether 'the Internet is more useful for work than for pleasure', here 52% of the respondents agreed, which is again a evidence for the trend of the Internet to become a commodity product in Germany.

In question 4 the respondents were asked about their time spending in front of the TV. The idea was to get information about the possibility that Digital TV (DTV) becomes a sales-medium for EC by its internet-connectivity. Therefore, the question was split into time spent in general (Q.4.a) and time spent alone in front of TV (Q.4.b). The thought was: if people shop over their DTV, they would do this mostly if using it alone like a computer. The results show that on average the respondents spent 8.6 hours per week in front of their TVs, 6 hours of them are watched alone (71%). If these numbers could be taken for granted, then DTV can be seen as a relatively good sales-medium following the outlined ideas, because most of the time in front of it is spent alone.

Next, question 5 and 6 focused on the internet-accessibility. In Question 5 the respondents were asked 'How useful would it be for you to access the Internet at public places'. This possibility was judged by 50% of the respondents with very important or important and by 17% with average.

The last question (Q.6) was focused on the aspect 'Thinking of the Internet as a giant shopping mall where you can buy and sell things'. The results of the sub-questions to

---

[29] People see the interactive household coming, but for themselves they stick to the well-known (the analogue TV).

question 6 are presented in Figure 24 on the next page. The results of these questions are only based on the replies of the e-mail and personal interview respondents (n=66), as the scale of this question in the web-page differed from the two others.

*Figure 24  Assessment of the Internet as a 'Shopping Mall'*

**Question 6 (e-mai and interview respondents)**

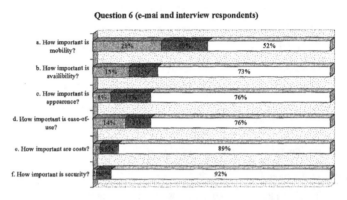

☐ very unimportant/unimportant  ☐ average  ☐ important/very important

Question 6 was also divided between 'internet-access respondents' and 'no internet-access respondents' but the results were relatively similar, except question 6.d, which was answered much more divergent (36% very important/important, 23% average) by the 'no internet-access respondents' (see Appendix B). Therefore, for the analyses of question 6 the two respondent-groups are summarised to one group. As can be seen from Figure 24, within the asked questions, question 6.a is the most divergent answered one, as only 52% see mobility as an important aspect to access the Internet for shopping. From this can be seen, that the current efforts of mobile phone producers and telephone companies to make palmtops and phones fit for the Internet, will most probably mainly be used for communication (e-mail, fax, information). All the other questions (Q.6.b-6.f) were answered by more than 75% of the respondents with very important or important. Especially the aspects 'ease-of-use' (Q.6.d), 'costs' (Q.6.e) and 'security' (Q.6.f) are seen by nearly all respondents as very important (see Appendix B). The importance of 'appearance' in the context of internet-shopping (Q.6.c) indicates the need for a sufficient screen-quality, especially on the new hand-helds, which have to be more than only bigger-sized screens of the current mobile phones.

## 3.6 Conclusion of Chapter 3: Where does Germany Stand?

This paragraph will draw a conclusion of the information found in the previous paragraphs of chapter 3. Furthermore, it will put the EC-use in Germany into the European context and compare Germany with other European countries and the US.

First of all, as mentioned in chapter 3.3.1 and which can also be seen from Appendix C, Germany finds itself in the European midfield concerning the use of the Internet. Compared to the US the gap becomes even bigger. Nevertheless, in the past EC sales had a huge growth rate, which was established by the *GfK Online-Monitor*. Books, CDs, flight- and journey-bookings had the strongest growth rate during the last 6 months (see chapter 3.3.2).

Europe's internet-demographics can be divided into three groups: the Nordic countries with the furthest grown penetration of internet- and mobile telephone users in the population, the Middle-European countries with a good established infrastructure and its dominating position, solely through its economic strength and population size, and last but not least the South-European countries, which are less well developed concerning the infrastructure but which had (and still have) the strongest growth-rate concerning the penetration of internet-users and access-devices in the population [AC99, p.20]. The German user-demographics are converging towards the average structure of the German population (see chapter 3.3.2). However, compared to the US user-demographics, Germany is still in the early adoption phase. For Europe as whole, Andersen Consulting found that: "European Internet users currently mirror the US early adopters of three to five years ago. European users are typically well educated, high-income, 30 year-old males employed either in academia or in the IT industry" [AC99, p.33].

Nevertheless, as described in chapter 3.2 the infrastructure for high quality EC applications like video-on-demand or Smart-Cards is existing in Germany. In the infrastructure section Germany finds itself within the top position in Europe and even holds a comparison with the US.

Just like the user-penteration of the Internet differs relatively strong between the European countries, the same hold for the different platforms of EC. "Italy, for instance, has only a small quota of its population computer-linked to the Internet, but has the largest number of mobile phones in Europe " [AC99, p.20]. Anderson Consulting found that Europe is more strongly positioned for future development of EC than its current performance might suggest. Especially the strong infrastructure and the use of future non-PC access-devices are seen as a powerful potential in which Europe could be ahead of the US. Already today, Europe is leading in the use of GSM mobile phones and Digital TV, as well as Smart-Cards. Through these devices EC will be (and increasingly is) conducted. These devices may absorb the lack of PC penetration compared to the US.

The results from the expert questionnaire show that EC is expected to have strong growth potentials (see chapter 3.4). The evaluation further exhibits that the EC's potentials are much more present and seen more homogeneous than its barriers, which are seen relatively divergent. Furthermore, the expert questionnaire indicates that the trend towards non-PC devices has started; the assessments of the different growth potentials are much more optimistic about these devices - the PCs is not any longer seen as *the* only EC access device.

The results from the general questionnaire indicate that the Internet and EC is seen by the respondents more open-minded than a lot of the studies might suggest. 37% of the respondents have already bought something online, 17% of them did so without a personal internet-access. Digital TV is seen by the respondents in the 'no internet-access' group as an alternative to a computer-access. Digital TV becomes even more interesting by the fact that 71% of the time in front of the TV is spent alone, which indicates that the TV can be used relatively similar to a computer. Furthermore, the idea of an 'interactive home' was not seen as a kind of science-fiction; 46% see this within 5 years to be a realistic development. As expected the points 'availability', 'appearance', 'ease-of-use', 'costs' and 'security' were judged by almost every respondent with very important or important.

# 4 Case Studies of Electronic Commerce Platforms

To get an idea of the discussed EC platforms and its growth-expectations, chapter 4 presents two case studies of EC platforms. The first one describes the Digital TV as a platform and outlines one possible application running on it. As an example, Galaxis' new Integrated Receiver Decoder and ZDF's Electronic Program Guide will be presented. The other case-study presents a Public Access Point tested since autumn 1998 by the Deutsche Telekom.

## 4.1 Galaxis' Integrated Receiver Decoder and ZDF's EPG

This case study of Galaxis' IQTV-IRD (Integrated Receiver Decoder) and ZDF's EPG (Elecronic Program Guide) should give an impression of the relatively new platform DTV as an EC access device, and furthermore present an application of DTV.

### 4.1.1 Galaxis' IQTV-IRD

Galaxis introduced its new IQTV-Integrated Receiver Decoder (IRD) in August 1998 at the Cebit Home in Hanover. Basis of this 'central multimedia terminal' is the open platform technology described in chapter 2.3 (see Figure 25).

*Figure 25 The Integrated Receiver Decoder, a Central Multimedia Terminal*

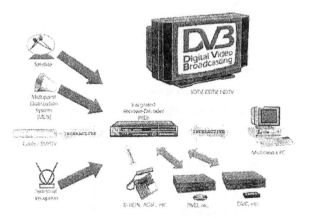

67

source: [GAL99]

The most important requirements of this IRD are described by Galaxis as follows [GAL98]:

- transcription of analogue audio- and video signals;

- communication with peripheral devices (TV, Video, Printer, PC, analogue SAT receiver, Hi-fi, modem, Keyboard, et.) at this the IRD functions as the 'central multimedia terminal';

- communication interfaces for multimedia applications like IEE 1394, common interface PCMCIA, IEEE 1284, Scart, RS232, etc.;

- graphical user interface (GUI);

- signal processing according to DVB MPEG-2 Standard;

- identification of the box in the net (addressability);

- ability to download applications and data, whereas the way of transmission should be irrelevant;

- security- and access-control for pay-TV and internet-access;

- provider-independent Common Access (CA) Interface (CI);

- hardware-independent API (for example Open TV).

The IRD is designed as an open platform concept that works on basis of the DVB common interface. The complete decryption is made by the CA module. Furthermore, the CI module contains a Smart-Card reader. The data-stream runs to the front end via the CI module and is encrypted and parsed by the ECM (Entitled Control Message) and EMM (Entitled Management Message) in the CA-demultiplex. The hierarchical structure or the Galaxis IQTV-IRD is presented in

Figure 26.

*Figure 26 Software Architecture of the Galaxis' IQTV-IRD*

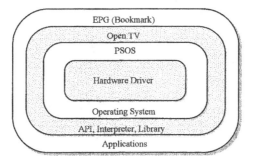

source: [GAL98]

Next an example for the application layer, the Electronic Program Guide of ZDF is presented in the following paragraph. It is only available with the Digital TV program of ZDF and ARD (not with their analogue programs).

### 4.1.2 ZDF's Electronic Program Guide

The Electronic Program Guide (EPG) from ZDF[30] is a further development of the common Video Text. It is only provided for the Digital TV division of ZDF's program and is converted via Digital TV set-top boxes like Galaxis IQTV-IRD, and is controlled via a remote control. Besides the EPG, ZDF's digital division provides interactive services like an online channel and Open TV as API.

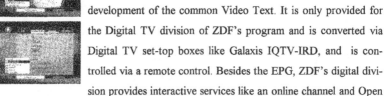

The EPG is organised in the sections *tip*, *preview*, *memo* and *menu* which are presented next [ZDF99].

*TV Tip* represents the former Video Text Information, enriched by notes to the ZDF.online program (web pages, audio- and video data).

---

[30] ZDF is the second public legal broadcaster in Germany.

*Preview* works like an electronic TV journal, it is organised by time and represents al digital TV programs of the ZDF group (Program Bouquets).

*Menu* searches the EPG for specific topics and presents them in an ordered list (all Sports, News, etc.).

*Memo* offers the possibility to arrange a personal TV program (profile), for example News, Crime Thriller, etc and list them under *my profile*.

The main advantages in contrast to the common Video Text can simply be characterised by the fact that the information gathering can be personalised through the user. This is the main difference of Digital TV, which was also described in chapter 2.3. Digital TV works from one-to-one not from one-to-many like in the past. Therefore applications like home-shopping or video-on-demand become possible. The navigation is organised via an intuitive user interface, the information can be arranged in differed graded depth.

### 4.1.3 Conclusion of the Galaxis' IRD and ZDF's EPG Case Study

The Galaxis IQTV-IRD has shown how non-PC devices can bring internet-content or

other online-services (like EPG) to the households. The aim is to split the basic functionality of the Internet (search, e-mail, information, etc.) from the technology-orientated devices like the PC which makes its handling more commode. The EPG is only one basic example of the way in which future EC applications could run on TVs; already today pay-per-view or different camera-perspectives in sport-events can be chosen in the digital pay TV program of DF1. As soon as Digital TV will broaden the mass, the TV program will change significantly. The normal TV program arranged by program-directors will have to compete with the programs on demand, in which the users become the 'program-directors'.

## 4.2  T-Kiosk from Deutsche Telekom

This paragraph outlines a pilot-project from Deutsche Telekom [TEL99], a Public Access Point (PAP), called T-Kiosk. The system provides the following functionality:

- telephone (standard and picture);

- fax;

- internet-access;

- e-mail;

- other services (nation-wide telephone-book, etc.).

These functions are controlled via a keyboard and a touch-screen. The PAP operates with all the major credit-cards and the telephone-card from Deutsche Telekom.

Figure 27 gives an impression of the appearance the T-Kiosk system.

*Figure 27 The Public Access Point from Deutsche Telekom*

The system will be placed in major cities in Germany, mainly at airports, train-stations and other places with high personal frequency. The T-Kiosk described in this paragraph is placed in the new shopping-mall 'Potsdammer Platz Arkarden' in Berlin. After naming the general features, the experiences with the e-mail and internet-access functionality will be described next in more detail, as the T-Kiosk system operates with a special surface, which differs from the common standard browser surfaces (Microsoft's Explorer or Netscape's Communicator).

### 4.2.1 Internet- and e-mail-Experiences with the T-Kiosk System

Before testing the system by myself, I tried to get additional information from Deutsche Telekom about systems placed, experiences and assessment of the future development of this project. Unfortunately, as the system is still in the pilot stage, non of the questions could be answered from Deutsche Telekom, either because of company confidentiality or because the project was not known within the companies public relations department. Therefore, this case study has to be based on user-experiences, in this case my own.

First of all it has to be mentioned that the interaction with the system is not as convenient as it should be for a PAP. The system is not able to distinguish between credit-card or telephone-card and the needed confirmation by the user is not intuitive. Next the switching from one service to another is also not quite intuitive, as several times the connection was closed although I just wanted to change from e-mail to Internet or fax. The same holds for the navigation within one application (because no mouse is integrated, the system has to be controlled with a touch pad similar to a notebook), which differs from the familiar navigation with a keyboard or mouse at a computer. Altogether, the system bears a lot of improving-potential to simplify the user interaction. After naming the disadvantages, the positive aspects of the system have to be mentioned as well.

The positive aspect of the system is without question the possibility to access the Internet or sent e-mails from a public place, without visiting an internet-cafe. Furthermore, the system embodies huge potentials, if believing the outlined future of Smart-Card usage of Schlumberger, described in chapter 1.5.2 (Smart-Cards), in which a personalised surface for every user through Smart-Card identification becomes possible.

Coming back to the reality of the present, the system operates with a reduced internet-browser and e-mail surface of t-online (the online service of Deutsche Telekom). The navigation works (if one gets used to the keyboard and touch pad) similar to the basic functionality of standard browsers and e-mail programs.[31]

### 4.2.2 Conclusion of the T-Kiosk from Deutsche Telekom Case Study

Concluding this case study, the costs for the user have to be mentioned as well. Also this aspect of the system is improvement worthy. The starting fee of 3.00 DM for the credit-card use is much to high, especially if encounting the various breakdowns caused of handling difficulties. The same holds for the operating fee of 0.30 DM per minute, which is extraordinary high facing the marginal costs of Internet and e-mail for the provider. Besides the too high costs, mentioned handling difficulty is a nega-

---

[31] A future question will be, whether people really need this e-mail surface or if they simply use their internet-e-mail provider (for example Yahoo or Hotmail).

tively point and needs to be improved. On the other side, Deutsche Telekom is on the right way and the outlined future of PAPs operating with Smart-Cards bears huge growth potentials for this system. Time will show how people adopt to the system.

# 5 Conclusion

The previous chapter of this study highlighted certain interesting aspects of the use of EC and the Internet, its current and future access-platforms and its position within Europe and in contrast to the US. Nonetheless in the fast changing world of EC, this study can only present a snap-shot of the current situation. Therefore, it is more important to focus on significant trends instead of concentrating on the pure numbers.

The study shows that in Germany EC is seen as an important aspect for future development of the economy. However, Germany is only positioned in the middle-field concerning internet-use, adoption-grade or internet-hosts per inhabitant. Against this, Germany is well positioned concerning high-quality infrastructure, for example the rate of digitalisation of the telephone-net or technologies like ISDN or ADSL (started last year).

The results of the expert questionnaire and the general questionnaire indicated that especially for the new EC platforms - Digital TV, mobile phone and Public Access Points - the assessments of its future development are very positive. Digital TV is seen by the 'no internet-access' group as a real alternative to a computer. Moreover, the results showed that the aspects 'availability', 'appearance', 'ease-of-use', 'costs' and 'security' are seen as a very important fact for the future success of EC.

To conclude this study with an outlook of EC trends, the focus is widen to the European perspective, as the way of use and the stage of EC in Europe differs fundamental to the US. If comparing Europe in concerns of PC-/internet-access-penetration, user-attitudes and sales-volume via telephone (which is mostly free in the local area in the US) paying with credit-cards, then the huge gap between US and EU is obvious. Against this, Dave Birch from Hyperion remarks: "If, however, we create a more open definition for this business tool [EC], then a very different picture emerges. The European application of electronic commerce is not only built to operate on the internet, but in the long term via GSM, digital TV and smart cards. And in all these areas, Europe is already leading the world market" [BIR99].

The development towards non-PC devices, that are easy to handle with specialised functionality will further push the use of EC applications, and lead to an overall higher percentage of internet-users via PC and non-PC devices. Through this trend the Internet could become an all-day commodity product like the TV or the telephone. Therefore in Europe a scenario becomes possible, in which EC and the use of the Internet is much more convenient than today. Its future commodity character enables to expand EC- and internet-services to a much broader mass (old people, kids, etc.) which do not have to be trained on how to operate a computer only to surf the web or send an e-mail. Therefore, if believing that the time of the powerful can-do-everything computer as *the* sole access-medium is slowly crumbling and other specialised devices will be used even more in the future, then Europe, and especially Germany, can be seen as relatively good positioned for the future of EC. However, the main drivers for EC will be the people's adoption speed of the new technologies and the regulatory authorities, which have to set convenient standards of EC but do not have to over-regulate the EC market, a still serious problem in the EU.

# Bibliography

[AC98]     Andersen Consulting (1998), eCommerce in Europe [pdf file],
           http://www.ac.com/sevices/ecommerce/ecommrept.pdf [accessed April
           15, 1999]

[BER99]    Berlin.de (1999), Homepage [web page], http://www.berlin.de
           [accessed June 5, 1999]

[BID99]    Birch, D. (April 1999), Does Europe mean e-business?,
           in: Ring, T. (Ed.), International Consultants' Guide - E-commerce,
           volume April 1999

[BJ99]     Brennan, J.D. (1999), Service-Centric Computing: The 21$^{st}$ Century
           Modell [pdf file], http://www.ac.com/services [accessed March 25,
           1999]

[BR98]     Bück, R. (October, 1998), Multimedia Home Platform [web page],
           http://www.digital-fernsehen.com/MHP/mhp.shtml [accessed April 21,
           1999]

[BRA99]    Brading, M. (April 1999), Fair Play, in: Ring, T. (Ed.), International
           Consultants' Guide - E-commerce, Volume April 1999

[CZ99a]    Computer Zeitung (February 18, 1999), Pakettechnik macht den Mo-
           bilfunk fit fürs Internet

[CZ99b]    Computer Zeitung (February 18, 1999), Mobilfunkbündnisse wollen
           dem Internet Beine machen

[CR99a]    Center for Research in Electronic Commerce UT Austin (1999), EC
           FAQ: What is Electronic Commerce? [web page],
           http://cism.bus.utexas.edu/resources/ecfaq/ecfaqa1.html [accessed
           April 8, 1999]

[CR99b]      Center for Research in Electronic Commerce UT Austin (1999), EC
             FAQ: web-storefronts [web page],
             http://cism.bus.utexas.edu/resources/ecfaq/ecfaqd2.html[accessed April
             8, 1999]

[CSWA98]     Choi, S./Whinston, A.B. (May 1998), Smart Cards: Enabling Smart
             Commerce in a Digital Age [web page],
             http://cism.bus.utexas.edu/works/articles/smartcardswp.html [accessed
             April 20, 1999]

[D2P99]      D2 privat (1999), Daten und Fakten zu D2 privat [web page],
             http://www.d2privat.de/presse/990316-presse-2.html [accessed June 5,
             1999]

[DTEL98]     Deutsche Telekom (1999), Geschäftsbericht 1998 [web page],
             http://www.dtag.de/untern/inv_relations/gesch_zahlen/geschaeft/98/ind
             ex.htm [accessed June 5, 1999]

[DTEL99]     Deutsche Telekom, (1999), Statistische Daten [web page],
             http://www.dtag.de/untern/inv_relations/gesch_zahlen/statistik/index.ht
             m [accessed June 5, 1999]

[DVB99a]     Digital Video Broadcasting Project (1999), DVB Standards [web
             page], http://www.dvb.org/dvb_side.htm [accessed April 21, 1999]

[DVB99b]     Digital Video Broadcasting Project (1999), Map of DVB standard
             adopted countries [web page], http://www.dvb.org/dvb_adopting.gif
             [accessed June 24, 1999]

[ECI99]      ECIN (March 24, 1999), Unternehmen im Internet [web page],
             http://www.ecin.de/marktbarometer/daten/unternehmen.html [Accessd
             April 12, 1999]

[ECM99]      e·Commerce Magazin (March/April 1999), Neue Wege ins digitale
             Kaufhaus, Volume 1/99

[EPLU99]     E Plus (1999), Kennzahlen [web page], http://www.eplus.de/haupt/
             fuersieueberuns/presse.htm#1[accessed June 5, 1999]

[ETO99a]    EU&ECC Statistics (1999), European Telework Development (ETD) [web page], http://www.eto.org.uk/eustats/penetr2.htm [accessed March 30, 1999]

[ETO99b]    EU&ECC Statistics (1999), Telecommunication and Penetration [web page], http://www.eto.org.uk/eustats/penetr.html [accessed June 20, 1999]

[FCC99]    Federal Communication Commission (1999), Home Page [web page], http://www.FFC.gov [accessed April 26, 1999]

[FOC99]    Focus Online (1999), Wie viele Menschen sind online? [web page], http://focus.de/dd36a.htm [accessed April 4, 1999]

[FOR99a]    Forrester Research ( January 1999), Howe, C.D., Nonstop eCommerce [pdf file], http://www.forrester.com/ER/Research/Report/ 0,1338,5708,FF.html [accessed April 6, 1999]

[FOR99b]    Forrester Research (January 1999), cited from Manager Magazin (March 1999, p.181)

[FUN99]    F.U.N. (1999), F.U.N. konkret [web page], http://www.fun-tv.de/funkonkret_7.htm [accessed April 21, 1999]

[GAL98]    Galaxis (August 1998), Galaxis Pressegespräch - Cebit Home, Hannover, PowerPoint slides received from Mrs. Kurtenbach (Stefan Susbauer marketing and communications)

[GAR99]    Gartner Research (May 5, 1999), Naqi J. , Microsoft Makes Stunning Moves in the Realm of Wireless [web page], http://www.gartner.com/advisory [accessed June 14, 1999]

[GfK99]    GfK (February 1999), GfK Online-Monitor - 3. Untersuchungswelle: Präsentation der zentralen Ergebnisse, Hamburg, PowerPoint slides recieved from Mr. Bronold (GfK)

[GP98]    Greenspun, P. (1998), Philip and Alex's Guide to Web Publishing: chapter 14 [web page], http://www.photo.net/wtr/thebook/ ecommerce.html [accessed April 14, 1999]

[GVU99]     (Graphics, Visualisation & Usability) Center of Georgia Tech Research
            Cooperation (1999), GVU's 10th WWW User Survey [web page],
            http://www.gvu.gatech.edu/user_surveys/survey-1998-10 [accessed
            April 2, 1999]

[IBM99]     IBM, IBM e-business [web page], http://www.ibm.com/e-
            business/index.html [accessed March 30, 1999]

[KRWA97]    Kalakota, R./Whinston, A.B. (1997), Electronic Commerce - A Man-
            ager's Guide, Addison Wesely

[KRWA99]    Kalakota, R./Whinston, A.B. , The Future of EDI on the Internet [web
            page] , http://cism.bus.utexas.edu/res/articles/commerce2.html
            [accessed March 27, 1999]

[KPMG98]    KPMG (1998), Electronic Commerce Research Report 1998 [pdf file],
            http://www.kpmg.com/ec_report.html [accessed March 26, 1999]

[NSF99]     NSF Workshop (January 25, 1999), Research Priorities in Electronic
            Commerce [web page], http://cism.bus.utexas.edu.workshop.
            ecdraft.html [accessed April 11, 1999]

[OECD98]    OECD (1998), Internet Infrastructure Indicators [pdf file],
            http://www.193.51.65.78/dsti/sti/it/cm/prod/tisp98-7e.pdf [accessed
            May 4, 1999]

[PIC90]     Picot, A./Dietl, H. (1990), Transaktionskostentheorie, WiSt,
            Volume 4

[PIC91]     Picot, A. (1991), Ökonomische Theorien der Organisation - Ein Über-
            blick über Ansätze und deren betriebswirtschaftliches Anwendungspo-
            tential, in: Büsselmann, E. (Ed.), Betriebswirtschaftslehre und ökono-
            mische Theorie, Stuttgart

[PLI95]     Plinke, W. (1995), Grundlagen des Business-to-Business-Marketing,
            in: Kleinaltenkamp, M./Plinke, W. (Ed.), Technischer Vertrieb:
            Grundlagen, Berlin et al.

[SLB99]      Schlumberger (1999), The Smart Village [web page],
             http://www.slb.com/smartcards/smart.html [accessed May 23, 1999]

[BID99]      Spottiswoode, A. (April 1999), Hidden Treasure, in: Ring, T. (Ed.),
             International Consultants' Guide - E-commerce, Volume April 1999

[TP99]       Timmers, P. (1999), Was bedeutet Electronic Commerce? [web page],
             http://www.eco.de/[ accessed April 12, 1999]

[VIA99]      Viag Interkom (1999), VIAG Interkom begrüßt 100.000sten Kunden
             im E2-Netz [web page], http://www2.viaginterkom.de/aps/presse/
             mitteilungen/news00448.html [accessed June 5, 1999]

[W3B99]      W3B (1999), Ergebnisse [web page], http://www.w3b.de/ergebnisse
             [accessed April 14, 1999]

[WIL85]      Williamson, O.E. (1985), The Economic Institutions of Capitalism,
             New York

[WSJE99a]    Wall Street Journal Europe, Strassel, K.A. (February 5, 1999),
             Bertelsmann Starts Online Bookstore

[WSJE99b]    Wall Street Journal Europe, Bransten, L. (March 5, 1999), Start-Up
             Firm AvantGo Aims to SoupUp Hand-Held Devices with Internet Data

[WSJE99c]    Wall Street Journal Europe, Bank, D. (February 9, 1999), Microsoft,
             BT to Develop Wireless Internet Service

[ZWA99]      Zwass, V. (1999), Structure and Macro-Level Impacts of Electronic
             Commerce: From Technological Infrastructure to Electronic Market-
             places [web page], http://www.mhhe.com/business/mis/
             zwass/ecpaper.html [accessed April 14, 1999]

# Appendix

## Appendix A: Expert Questionnaire

**Expert Questionnaire**

# Fragebogen zur Diplomarbeit

Electronic Commerce über unterschiedliche Plattformen

- eine europäische Studie der Nutzung von Electronic Commerce -

von Stephan Siehl

Bitte beantworten Sie die folgenden Fragen:

**Welcher Abteilung gehören Sie an?**  Management/Marketing ☐

IT ☐

andere _____

_____

**1. Wie schätzen Sie allgemein die Potentiale von Electronic Commerce ein?**

| | stark | | | | schwach |
|---|---|---|---|---|---|
| 1. **Interprozeßoptimierung** (Business to Business) | ☐ | ☐ | ☐ | ☐ | ☐ |
| 2. **Intraprozeßoptimierung** (Workflow) | ☐ | ☐ | ☐ | ☐ | ☐ |
| 3. Produktpräsentation/-information | ☐ | ☐ | ☐ | ☐ | ☐ |
| 4. Absatz/Vertrieb | ☐ | ☐ | ☐ | ☐ | ☐ |
| 5. Optimierung des Zahlungsverkehrs | ☐ | ☐ | ☐ | ☐ | ☐ |
| 6. andere, _____ | ☐ | ☐ | ☐ | ☐ | ☐ |

**2. a) Haben Sie bereits Electronic Commerce in Ihrem Unternehmen implementiert?**

☐ Ja ☐ Nein

**b) Falls Nein, Planen Sie Electronic Commerce in Ihrem Unternehmen zu implementieren?**

☐ Ja, und zwar in den nächtens 6 Monaten ☐ Nein

☐ 12 Monaten

☐ später

**3. Die Folgenden Fragen beziehen sich auf Ihre persönlichen Einschätzungen**

| | Ja | Nein |
|---|---|---|
| 1. Mobiltelefone werden in Zukunft verstärkt für electronic commerce genutzt | ☐ | ☐ |
| 2. Digital TV wird in Zukunft verstärkt für electronic commerce genutzt | ☐ | ☐ |
| 3. Öffentliche Internetzugänge werden in Zukunft verstärkt für electronic commerce genutzt | ☐ | ☐ |

4. Wäre das Internet „einfacher" so würde mehr darüber gekauft ☐ ☐

5. Der vernetzte Haushalt wird schon bald Realität sein (Waschmaschine an das Internet angeschlossen o.ä.) ☐ ☐

**4. a) Bietet Ihr Unternehmen Electronic Commerce Technologien an?**

☐ Ja    ☐ Nein

**b) Wenn Ja, in welchem Bereich(en)?**

☐ Computer

☐ Netzzugang (Internet/Telefon)

☐ Mobiltelefon

☐ Digital TV

☐ Hand-Devices

☐ Zugangshardware (Terminals etc.)

☐ andere, und zwar _____

**5. Wie schätzt Ihr Unternehmen die Entwicklung in den folgenden Bereichen ein?**
(Beantworten Sie nur Prognosen für Bereiche, die für Ihre Firma relevant sind)

1. **Ende des Jahres** werden in Deutschland _____ Million Haushalte einen **PC** besitzen. Im Jahr **2003** werden es _____ Million sein.

2. **Ende des Jahres** werden in Deutschland _____ Million Haushalte **Internetzugang** haben. Im Jahr **2003** werden es _____ Million sein.

3. **Ende des Jahres** werden in Deutschland _____ Million Personen ein **Mobiltelefon** besitzen. Im Jahr **2003** werden es _____ Million sein.

4. **Ende des Jahres** werden in Deutschland _____ Million Haushalte einen **Digital TV** Anschluß haben. Im Jahr **2003** werden es _____ Million sein.

5. **Ende des Jahres** wird es in Deutschland _____ Million **öffentliche Internet-Terminals** geben. Im Jahr **2003** werden es _____ Million sein.

**6. Was sind Ihrer Meinung nach die größten Hemmnisse für Electronic Commerce in Deutschland?**

|  | trifft zu |  |  |  | trifft nicht zu |  |
|---|---|---|---|---|---|---|
| 1. Sicherheit der Zahlung | | ☐ | ☐ | ☐ | ☐ | ☐ |
| 2. Mangelnde Authentizität der Geschäftspartner | ☐ | ☐ | ☐ | ☐ | ☐ | |
| 3. Komplizierte Handhabung | ☐ | ☐ | ☐ | ☐ | ☐ | |
| 4. Hohe Telefongebühren | ☐ | ☐ | ☐ | ☐ | ☐ | |

5. Zu geringe Penetration in
   Bevölkerung
   
   ☐ ☐ ☐ ☐ ☐

6. Annonymitätsverlangen der
   der Nutzer
   
   ☐ ☐ ☐ ☐ ☐

*Tab. 2 Results of the Expert Questionnaire*

| Number | Company | Devision | 1.1 | 1.2 | 1.3 | 1.4 | 1.5 | 2a | 2b | 3.1 | 3.2 | 3.3 | 3.4 | 3.5 | 4a | 4b1 | 4b2 | 4b3 | 4b4 | 4b5 | 4b6 | 4b7 | 6.1 | 6.2 | 6.3 | 6.4 | 6.5 | 6.6 |
|---|---|---|---|---|---|---|---|---|---|---|---|---|---|---|---|---|---|---|---|---|---|---|---|---|---|---|---|---|
| 1 | Telekom | 1 | 5 | 5 | 5 | 5 | 5 | 1 | | 1 | 1 | 1 | 1 | 1 | 1 | 0 | 0 | 0 | 0 | 0 | 0 | 1 | 2 | 1 | 1 | 5 | 2 | 2 |
| 2 | IBM | 1 | 5 | 5 | 5 | 5 | 5 | 1 | | 1 | 1 | 1 | 1 | 1 | 1 | 0 | 0 | 0 | 0 | 0 | 0 | 1 | 2 | 1 | 4 | 3 | 4 | 2 |
| 3 | | 1 | 5 | 5 | 5 | 4 | 5 | 1 | | 1 | 1 | 1 | 1 | 0 | 1 | 0 | 0 | 0 | 0 | 0 | 0 | 0 | 1 | 3 | 3 | 3 | 4 | 4 |
| 4 | | 1 | 5 | 5 | 4 | 3 | 1 | 1 | | 1 | 1 | 1 | 1 | 1 | 0 | 0 | 0 | 0 | 0 | 0 | 0 | 1 | 4 | 4 | 5 | 4 | 5 | 5 |
| 5 | | 1 | 4 | 3 | 4 | 5 | 1 | 0 | | 1 | 1 | 1 | 1 | 0 | 1 | 1 | 0 | 0 | 0 | 0 | 0 | 0 | 3 | 3 | 5 | 5 | 3 | 3 |
| 6 | | 1 | 3 | 4 | 3 | 5 | 1 | 1 | | 1 | 1 | 1 | 0 | 0 | 0 | 0 | 0 | 0 | 0 | 0 | 0 | 0 | 2 | 1 | 2 | 4 | 3 | 4 |
| 7 | ECO | 1 | 5 | 5 | 5 | 4 | 0 | 1 | | 1 | 1 | 1 | 1 | 1 | 1 | 0 | 0 | 0 | 0 | 0 | 0 | 0 | 5 | 4 | 5 | 5 | 4 | 3 |
| 8 | | 1 | 5 | 5 | 5 | 4 | 1 | 0 | 1 | 1 | 1 | 1 | 0 | 1 | 0 | 0 | 0 | 0 | 0 | 0 | 0 | 1 | 4 | 3 | 4 | 5 | 4 | 3 |
| 9 | GfK | 1 | 5 | 5 | 4 | 4 | 1 | 0 | | 1 | 1 | 1 | 0 | 0 | 0 | 0 | 0 | 0 | 0 | 0 | 0 | 0 | 4 | 4 | 5 | 5 | 5 | 4 |
| 10 | ZDF | 1 | 5 | 5 | 4 | 5 | 0 | 2 | | 1 | 1 | 1 | 0 | 1 | 1 | 0 | 0 | 0 | 0 | 0 | 0 | 1 | 5 | 3 | 5 | 5 | 5 | 5 |
| 11 | | 2 | 4 | 4 | 4 | 4 | 1 | 1 | 1 | 1 | 1 | 1 | 1 | 0 | 0 | 0 | 0 | 0 | 0 | 0 | 0 | 0 | 2 | 3 | 1 | 1 | 3 | 3 |
| 12 | | 1 | 5 | 5 | 4 | 4 | 1 | 0 | | 1 | 1 | 1 | 1 | 0 | 0 | 0 | 0 | 0 | 0 | 0 | 0 | 0 | 2 | 4 | 3 | 2 | 4 | 2 |
| 13 | | 1 | 5 | 5 | 4 | 3 | 1 | 0 | | 1 | 1 | 0 | 0 | 0 | 0 | 0 | 0 | 0 | 0 | 0 | 0 | 0 | 3 | 3 | 3 | 2 | 4 | 2 |
| 14 | | 1 | 5 | 5 | 4 | 2 | 1 | 1 | | 1 | 1 | 0 | 0 | 1 | 1 | 0 | 0 | 0 | 0 | 0 | 0 | 0 | 4 | 4 | 2 | 3 | 4 | 5 |
| 15 | | 2 | 4 | 4 | 5 | 1 | 0 | 0 | | 1 | 1 | 1 | 1 | 0 | 1 | 0 | 0 | 0 | 0 | 0 | 0 | 1 | 5 | 3 | 3 | 4 | 4 | 4 |
| 16 | | 2 | 5 | 4 | 5 | 2 | 0 | 1 | | 1 | 1 | 0 | 1 | 0 | 0 | 0 | 1 | 0 | 0 | 0 | 0 | 1 | 4 | 4 | 3 | 5 | 3 | 4 |
| 17 | | 1 | 5 | 4 | 4 | 1 | 0 | 1 | | 1 | 1 | 0 | 1 | 0 | 0 | 0 | 0 | 0 | 0 | 0 | 0 | 0 | 4 | 4 | 2 | 4 | 4 | 4 |
| 18 | | 1 | 4 | 3 | 3 | 5 | 0 | 1 | | 1 | 1 | 1 | 1 | 1 | 0 | 0 | 0 | 0 | 0 | 1 | 0 | 0 | 5 | 3 | 5 | 5 | 3 | 4 |
| 19 | | 1 | 2 | 2 | 4 | 1 | 0 | 0 | | 1 | 1 | 0 | 1 | 0 | 0 | 0 | 0 | 0 | 0 | 0 | 0 | 0 | 2 | 3 | 5 | 5 | 4 | 4 |
| 20 | | 1 | 5 | 5 | 5 | 5 | 1 | 0 | | 1 | 1 | 1 | 1 | 0 | 1 | 0 | 1 | 1 | 0 | 0 | 0 | 1 | 4 | 3 | 5 | 5 | 5 | 3 |
| 21 | | 1 | 5 | 5 | 4 | 4 | 1 | 0 | | 1 | 1 | 1 | 1 | 1 | 0 | 0 | 1 | 1 | 0 | 0 | 0 | 0 | 4 | 4 | 4 | 3 | 4 | 3 |
| 22 | | 1 | 5 | 5 | 5 | 3 | 1 | 0 | 3 | 1 | 1 | 1 | 1 | 0 | 0 | 0 | 0 | 0 | 0 | 0 | 0 | 0 | 1 | 3 | 3 | 5 | 3 | 1 |
| 23 | Novalabs | 2 | 2 | 2 | 2 | 3 | 1 | 0 | | 1 | 1 | 1 | 1 | 1 | 1 | 0 | 0 | 0 | 0 | 0 | 0 | 0 | 5 | 4 | 1 | 1 | 4 | 1 |
| 24 | | 2 | 5 | 5 | 5 | 5 | 0 | 0 | | 1 | 1 | 1 | 1 | 1 | 1 | 0 | 0 | 1 | 1 | 0 | 0 | 0 | 4 | 5 | 2 | 4 | 4 | 4 |
| 25 | | 3 | 4 | 2 | 3 | 4 | 1 | 0 | | 1 | 1 | 1 | 1 | 0 | 0 | 0 | 0 | 0 | 1 | 0 | 0 | 1 | 4 | 4 | 4 | 4 | 4 | 2 |
| 26 | | 3 | 5 | 5 | 4 | 3 | 1 | 0 | | 1 | 1 | 1 | 0 | 1 | 1 | 0 | 0 | 0 | 0 | 0 | 1 | 0 | 5 | 1 | 5 | 5 | 5 | 5 |
| 27 | | 3 | 2 | 2 | 4 | 5 | 1 | 0 | | 1 | 1 | 1 | 1 | 1 | 0 | 1 | 0 | 1 | 0 | 1 | 0 | 0 | 5 | 4 | 2 | 4 | 4 | 4 |
| 28 | Acor | 2 | 4 | 4 | 4 | 3 | 1 | 1 | | 1 | 1 | 1 | 1 | 0 | 0 | 0 | 0 | 0 | 0 | 1 | 0 | 1 | 5 | 3 | 4 | 4 | 3 | 3 |
| 29 | | 3 | 5 | 5 | 4 | 4 | 1 | 0 | | 1 | 1 | 0 | 1 | 1 | 1 | 0 | 1 | 0 | 0 | 0 | 0 | 0 | 3 | 3 | 1 | 1 | 3 | 3 |
| 30 | Infomatec | 3 | 5 | 4 | 2 | 3 | 1 | 0 | | 1 | 1 | 1 | 1 | 0 | 0 | 0 | 0 | 1 | 0 | 1 | 0 | 1 | 4 | 4 | 5 | 4 | 4 | 2 |
| 31 | Microsoft | 3 | 5 | 5 | 4 | 4 | 1 | 0 | | 1 | 1 | 1 | 1 | 1 | 1 | 1 | 1 | 0 | 1 | 0 | 0 | 0 | 1 | 2 | 4 | 5 | 3 | 4 |
| 32 | | 3 | 5 | 5 | 4 | 5 | 1 | 0 | | 1 | 1 | 1 | 0 | 0 | 0 | 0 | 0 | 0 | 0 | 1 | 0 | 1 | 2 | 2 | 3 | 4 | 3 | 3 |
| 33 | ECRC | 3 | 5 | 4 | 4 | 5 | 1 | 0 | | 0 | 1 | 0 | 1 | 1 | 1 | 0 | 0 | 0 | 0 | 1 | 0 | 1 | 5 | 5 | 1 | 5 | 3 | 4 |
| 34 | | 3 | 5 | 5 | 4 | 5 | 1 | 0 | | 1 | 1 | 1 | 1 | 0 | 1 | 0 | 0 | 0 | 0 | 0 | 0 | 2 | 5 | 5 | 3 | 5 | 3 | 3 |
| 35 | | 3 | 5 | 5 | 5 | 5 | 1 | 0 | | 1 | 1 | 1 | 1 | 1 | 1 | 0 | 0 | 0 | 0 | 0 | 0 | 5 | 2 | 3 | 3 | 5 | 3 | 3 |
| 36 | | 3 | 4 | 4 | 4 | 4 | 1 | 0 | | 1 | 1 | 0 | 1 | 0 | 0 | 1 | 1 | 1 | 1 | 0 | 0 | 5 | 5 | 3 | 3 | 5 | 3 | 3 |
| | **Mean** | | 4,32 | 4,3 | 4,22 | 3,86 | 3,78 | 0,67 | | 0,81 | 0,89 | 0,86 | 0,78 | 0,7 | 0,72 | 0,21 | 0,5 | 0,21 | 0,36 | 0,07 | 0,21 | 0,64 | 4,19 | 3,41 | 3,32 | 3,62 | 3,92 | 3,57 |
| | **Variance** | | 1,4 | 1 | 0,7 | 1,2 | 2,4 | 0,2 | | 0,2 | 0,2 | 0,2 | 0,2 | 0,3 | 0,2 | 0,3 | 0,3 | 0,3 | 0,3 | 0,1 | 0,2 | 0,3 | 1,8 | 1,3 | 2,3 | 2,5 | 1,9 | 1,3 |

**Appendix B: General Questionnaire**

# Fragebogen

### Electronic Commerce über unterschiedliche Plattformen
- eine europäische Studie der Nutzung von Electronic Commerce -

#### von Stephan Siehl

Bitte beantworten Sie die folgenden Fragen:

**1. Haben Sie zu Hause oder auf der Arbeit Internet-Zugang?** ☐ Ja ☐ Nein

**2. Haben Sie bereits Produkte/DL über das Internet gekauft?** ☐ Ja ☐ Nein

**3. Sind die folgenden Aussagen Ihrer Meinung nach richtig oder falsch?**

|  | Ja | Nein |
|---|---|---|
| 3.a Das Internet ist kompliziert, und Einkaufen darüber erst recht. | ☐ | ☐ |
| 3.b In 5 Jahren wird der „interaktive Haushalt", mit verschiedenen Haushaltsgeräten angeschlossen an das Internet, Realität sein. | ☐ | ☐ |
| 3.c Die Möglichkeit Produkte/DL vom Sofa aus zu kaufen ist Grund genug ein Digital TV (Set) zu kaufen. | ☐ | ☐ |
| 3.d Das Internet ist nützlicher für die Arbeit als für die Freizeit. | ☐ | ☐ |

**4.a Wieviel Stunden verbringen Sie pro Woche vor dem Fernseher?** Stunden
**4.b Wieviel Stunden davon alleine?** Stunden

|  | wichtig |  |  | unwichtig |
|---|---|---|---|---|
| **5. Wie nützlich währe für Sie die Möglichkeit das** ☐ | ☐ | ☐ | ☐ | ☐ |

**Internet von öffentlichen Plätzen wie z.B. Einkaufszentren, Bahnstationen, Internet Cafés aus zu erreichen.**

**6. Das Internet als ein großes Einkaufszentrum, in dem Waren ge- und verkauft werden.**

|  | wichtig |  |  |  | unwichtig |
|---|---|---|---|---|---|
| 6.a Wie wichtig ist Mobilität? (Internet-Zugang kann überall hin mitgenommen werden) | ☐ | ☐ | ☐ | ☐ | ☐ |
| 6.b Wie wichtig ist öffentlicher Zugang/Verfügbarkeit? | ☐ | ☐ | ☐ | ☐ | ☐ |
| 6.c Wie wichtig ist die Qualität der Darstellung? | ☐ | ☐ | ☐ | ☐ | ☐ |
| 6.d Wie wichtig ist einfache Handhabung? | ☐ | ☐ | ☐ | ☐ | ☐ |
| 6.e Wie wichtig sind Kosten (Anschaffung/Zugang) | ☐ | ☐ | ☐ | ☐ | ☐ |
| 6.d Wie wichtig ist Sicherheit (Transaktion, ☐Datenschutz usw.) | | ☐ | ☐ | ☐ | ☐ |

## Results of the General Questionnaire

*Tab. 3 Results of the General Questionnaire*

| Number | Respond | 1 | 2 | 3.a | 3.b | 3.c | 3.d | 4.a | 4.b | 5 | 6.a | 6.b | 6.c | 6.d | 6.e | 6.f |
|---|---|---|---|---|---|---|---|---|---|---|---|---|---|---|---|---|
| 1 | e-mail | 0 | 0 | 0 | 1 | 1 | 1 | 2 | 0 | 5 | 5 | 5 | 5 | 5 | 5 | 5 |
| 2 | e-mail | 1 | 1 | 0 | 0 | 0 | 0 | 1 | 1 | 5 | 5 | 5 | 5 | 5 | 3 | 5 |
| 3 | e-mail | 1 | 0 | 1 | 1 | 0 | 1 | 0 | 0 | 3 | 2 | 5 | 5 | 5 | 5 | 5 |
| 4 | e-mail | 1 | 0 | 0 | 0 | 0 | 1 | 14 | 12 | 2 | 2 | 4 | 4 | 5 | 4 | 5 |
| 5 | e-mail | 1 | 1 | 0 | 1 | 0 | 1 | 5 | 3 | 5 | 5 | 5 | 3 | 4 | 4 | 5 |
| 6 | e-mail | 1 | 1 | 0 | 0 | 0 | 1 | 7 | 1 | 5 | 5 | 5 | 5 | 5 | 5 | 5 |
| 7 | e-mail | 1 | 0 | 1 | 0 | 0 | 1 | 9 | 5 | 1 | 5 | 5 | 5 | 5 | 5 | 5 |
| 8 | e-mail | 1 | 1 | 0 | 0 | 0 | 1 | 7,5 | 3,5 | 2 | 2 | 4 | 5 | 5 | 5 | 4 |
| 9 | e-mail | 1 | 1 | 0 | 0 | 0 | 0 | 3 | 1,5 | 1 | 3 | 5 | 5 | 5 | 5 | 5 |
| 10 | e-mail | 1 | 0 | 0 | 0 | 0 | 0 | 42 | 35 | 2 | 3 | 4 | 5 | 5 | 5 | 4 |
| 11 | e-mail | 1 | 0 | 0 | 1 | 0 | 0 | 20 | 15 | 4 | 5 | 4 | 3 | 5 | 5 | 5 |
| 12 | e-mail | 1 | 1 | 0 | 0 | 0 | 0 | 2 | 1 | 5 | 5 | 5 | 3 | 5 | 5 | 5 |
| 13 | e-mail | 1 | 0 | 0 | 1 | 0 | 0 | 4 | 3 | 4 | 3 | 4 | 5 | 5 | 5 | 5 |
| 14 | e-mail | 1 | 0 | 0 | 0 | 1 | 0 | 14 | 13 | 4 | 4 | 4 | 5 | 5 | 5 | 5 |
| 15 | e-mail | 1 | 0 | 0 | 1 | 0 | 0 | 5 | 3,5 | 4 | 4 | 4 | 5 | 4 | 4 | 5 |
| 16 | e-mail | 1 | 1 | 0 | 1 | 0 | 1 | 4 | 0 | 1 | 3 | 2 | 5 | 5 | 5 | 5 |
| 17 | e-mail | 1 | 0 | 0 | 1 | 0 | 1 | 6 | 6 | 2 | 1 | 1 | 5 | 5 | 5 | 5 |
| 18 | e-mail | 1 | 1 | 0 | 0 | 0 | 0 | 1 | 1 | 5 | 5 | 5 | 5 | 5 | 3 | 5 |
| 19 | e-mail | 1 | 0 | 1 | 1 | 0 | 1 | 0 | 0 | 3 | 2 | 5 | 5 | 5 | 5 | 5 |
| 20 | e-mail | 1 | 0 | 0 | 0 | 0 | 1 | 14 | 12 | 2 | 2 | 4 | 4 | 5 | 4 | 5 |
| 21 | e-mail | 1 | 1 | 0 | 1 | 0 | 1 | 5 | 3 | 5 | 5 | 5 | 3 | 4 | 4 | 5 |
| 22 | e-mail | 1 | 1 | 0 | 0 | 0 | 1 | 7 | 1 | 5 | 5 | 5 | 5 | 5 | 5 | 5 |
| 23 | e-mail | 1 | 0 | 1 | 0 | 0 | 1 | 9 | 5 | 1 | 5 | 5 | 5 | 5 | 5 | 5 |
| 24 | e-mail | 1 | 1 | 0 | 0 | 0 | 1 | 7 | 4 | 2 | 2 | 4 | 5 | 5 | 5 | 4 |
| 25 | e-mail | 1 | 1 | 0 | 0 | 0 | 0 | 3 | 2,5 | 1 | 3 | 5 | 5 | 5 | 5 | 5 |
| 26 | Interview | 0 | 0 | 0 | 1 | 1 | 1 | 2 | 0 | 5 | 5 | 5 | 5 | 4 | 5 | 5 |
| 27 | Interview | 0 | 0 | 0 | 0 | 1 | 1 | 15 | 10 | 1 | 4 | 5 | 2 | 2 | 4 | 5 |
| 28 | Interview | 0 | 0 | 1 | 0 | 0 | 1 | 5 | 2 | 1 | 1 | 1 | 1 | 1 | 1 | 1 |
| 29 | Interview | 0 | 0 | 0 | 0 | 1 | 0 | 6 | 5 | 4 | 3 | 4 | 5 | 5 | 5 | 5 |
| 30 | Interview | 0 | 0 | 1 | 0 | 0 | 0 | 20 | 15 | 1 | 1 | 3 | 1 | 1 | 5 | 5 |
| 31 | Interview | 0 | 0 | 0 | 0 | 0 | 1 | 17 | 5 | 5 | 4 | 3 | 5 | 2 | 4 | 4 |
| 32 | Interview | 0 | 0 | 0 | 1 | 0 | 0 | 5 | 5 | 3 | 3 | 4 | 4 | 2 | 5 | 5 |
| 33 | Interview | 0 | 0 | 0 | 0 | 0 | 0 | 10 | 8 | 1 | 1 | 1 | 5 | 1 | 4 | 4 |
| 34 | Interview | 0 | 0 | 0 | 0 | 1 | 1 | 15 | 5 | 4 | 3 | 4 | 5 | 5 | 5 | 5 |
| 35 | Interview | 0 | 0 | 1 | 0 | 0 | 1 | 15 | 15 | 1 | 1 | 3 | 3 | 3 | 5 | 4 |
| 36 | Interview | 0 | 0 | 0 | 0 | 1 | 0 | 10 | 5 | 5 | 4 | 5 | 4 | 4 | 4 | 5 |
| 37 | Interview | 0 | 0 | 0 | 1 | 0 | 1 | 20 | 20 | 2 | 2 | 4 | 3 | 3 | 4 | 3 |
| 38 | Interview | 0 | 1 | 1 | 1 | 1 | 1 | 10 | 9 | 5 | 4 | 5 | 5 | 4 | 5 | 5 |
| 39 | Interview | 0 | 1 | 0 | 1 | 0 | 1 | 13 | 10 | 3 | 2 | 2 | 4 | 2 | 3 | 3 |
| 40 | Interview | 0 | 0 | 0 | 0 | 1 | 0 | 2 | 0 | 5 | 4 | 5 | 5 | 5 | 5 | 5 |
| 41 | Interview | 0 | 1 | 1 | 0 | 0 | 1 | 15 | 5 | 3 | 5 | 3 | 2 | 3 | 3 | 4 |
| 42 | Interview | 0 | 0 | 1 | 0 | 1 | 0 | 10 | 10 | 5 | 1 | 2 | 4 | 3 | 5 | 5 |
| 43 | Interview | 0 | 0 | 0 | 1 | 1 | 1 | 5 | 5 | 3 | 3 | 5 | 3 | 2 | 2 | 5 |
| 44 | Interview | 0 | 0 | 1 | 0 | 0 | 1 | 10 | 7 | 5 | 4 | 3 | 5 | 4 | 4 | 5 |
| 45 | Interview | 0 | 0 | 0 | 1 | 0 | 0 | 5 | 0 | 3 | 5 | 4 | 5 | 5 | 5 | 5 |
| 46 | Interview | 0 | 0 | 0 | 0 | 1 | 0 | 10 | 8 | 5 | 3 | 5 | 3 | 3 | 4 | 5 |
| 47 | Interview | 1 | 0 | 0 | 0 | 0 | 0 | 20 | 10 | 2 | 3 | 4 | 5 | 5 | 5 | 4 |
| 48 | Interview | 1 | 0 | 0 | 1 | 0 | 0 | 35 | 30 | 4 | 5 | 4 | 3 | 5 | 5 | 5 |
| 49 | Interview | 1 | 1 | 0 | 0 | 0 | 0 | 2 | 1 | 5 | 5 | 5 | 3 | 5 | 5 | 5 |
| 50 | Interview | 1 | 0 | 0 | 1 | 0 | 0 | 4 | 3 | 4 | 3 | 4 | 5 | 5 | 5 | 5 |
| 51 | Interview | 1 | 0 | 0 | 0 | 1 | 0 | 14 | 13 | 4 | 4 | 4 | 5 | 5 | 5 | 5 |
| 52 | Interview | 1 | 0 | 0 | 1 | 0 | 0 | 5 | 3,5 | 4 | 4 | 4 | 5 | 3 | 4 | 5 |
| 53 | Interview | 1 | 1 | 0 | 1 | 0 | 1 | 4 | 0 | 1 | 3 | 2 | 5 | 5 | 5 | 5 |
| 54 | Interview | 1 | 0 | 0 | 1 | 0 | 1 | 6 | 6 | 2 | 1 | 1 | 5 | 5 | 5 | 5 |
| 55 | Interview | 1 | 0 | 1 | 0 | 0 | 1 | 10 | 6 | 4 | 2 | 3 | 4 | 5 | 5 | 5 |
|  | Interview | 1 | 0 | 0 | 0 | 1 | 1 | 8 | 8 | 2 | 2 | 3 | 4 | 5 | 5 | 5 |

| Number | Respond | 1 | 2 | 3.a | 3.b | 3.c | 3.d | 4.a | 4.b | 5 | 6.a | 6.b | 6.c | 6.d | 6.e | 6.f |
|---|---|---|---|---|---|---|---|---|---|---|---|---|---|---|---|---|
| 56 | Interview | 1 | 1 | 0 | 1 | 0 | 0 | 5 | 5 | 5 | 5 | 5 | 5 | 5 | 5 | 5 |
| 57 | Interview | 1 | 1 | 0 | 1 | 1 | 1 | 2 | 2 | 3 | 4 | 2 | 2 | 5 | 5 | 5 |
| 58 | Interview | 1 | 0 | 0 | 0 | 1 | 1 | 10 | 8 | 4 | 4 | 4 | 5 | 3 | 4 | 5 |
| 59 | Interview | 1 | 0 | 1 | 0 | 0 | 0 | 8 | 5 | 1 | 1 | 4 | 3 | 2 | 4 | 5 |
| 60 | Interview | 1 | 0 | 0 | 1 | 1 | 1 | 4 | 4 | 4 | 4 | 5 | 5 | 5 | 4 | 4 |
| 61 | Interview | 1 | 0 | 0 | 0 | 1 | 0 | 14 | 13 | 4 | 4 | 4 | 5 | 5 | 5 | 5 |
| 62 | Interview | 1 | 0 | 0 | 1 | 1 | 0 | 5 | 3 | 3 | 2 | 2 | 4 | 4 | 3 | 3 |
| 63 | Interview | 1 | 1 | 1 | 1 | 0 | 1 | 12 | 8 | 3 | 5 | 3 | 5 | 4 | 5 | 4 |
| 64 | Interview | 1 | 0 | 1 | 0 | 0 | 0 | 30 | 25 | 5 | 5 | 4 | 5 | 4 | 4 | 3 |
| 65 | Interview | 1 | 0 | 1 | 1 | 0 | 1 | 5 | 0 | 3 | 5 | 4 | 5 | 5 | 5 | 5 |
| 66 | web page | 1 | 1 | 1 | 1 | 0 | 1 | 0 | 0 | n.d. | n.d. | n.d. | n.d. | n.d. | n.d. | n.d. |
| 67 | web page | 1 | 1 | 1 | 0 | 0 | 0 | 10 | 8 | n.d. | n.d. | n.d. | n.d. | n.d. | n.d. | n.d. |
| 68 | web page | 1 | 1 | 0 | 1 | 0 | 1 | 5 | 3 | n.d. | n.d. | n.d. | n.d. | n.d. | n.d. | n.d. |
| 69 | web page | 1 | 0 | 0 | 0 | 0 | 1 | 1 | 0 | n.d. | n.d. | n.d. | n.d. | n.d. | n.d. | n.d. |
| 70 | web page | 1 | 0 | 0 | 0 | 1 | 0 | 25 | 18 | n.d. | n.d. | n.d. | n.d. | n.d. | n.d. | n.d. |
| 71 | web page | 1 | 1 | 0 | 1 | 1 | 1 | 8 | 8 | n.d. | n.d. | n.d. | n.d. | n.d. | n.d. | n.d. |
| 72 | web page | 1 | 1 | 0 | 1 | 0 | 1 | 5 | 4 | n.d. | n.d. | n.d. | n.d. | n.d. | n.d. | n.d. |
| 73 | web page | 1 | 0 | 0 | 0 | 0 | 0 | 15 | 8 | n.d. | n.d. | n.d. | n.d. | n.d. | n.d. | n.d. |
| 74 | web page | 1 | 1 | 0 | 1 | 0 | 0 | 6 | 3 | n.d. | n.d. | n.d. | n.d. | n.d. | n.d. | n.d. |
| 75 | web page | 1 | 1 | 0 | 1 | 0 | 0 | 5 | 4 | n.d. | n.d. | n.d. | n.d. | n.d. | n.d. | n.d. |
| 76 | web page | 1 | 0 | 1 | 1 | 0 | 0 | 5 | 4 | n.d. | n.d. | n.d. | n.d. | n.d. | n.d. | n.d. |
| 77 | web page | 1 | 0 | 0 | 0 | 0 | 0 | 6 | 4 | n.d. | n.d. | n.d. | n.d. | n.d. | n.d. | n.d. |
| 78 | web page | 0 | 1 | 0 | 1 | 0 | 0 | 0 | 0 | n.d. | n.d. | n.d. | n.d. | n.d. | n.d. | n.d. |
| 79 | web page | 1 | 1 | 1 | 1 | 0 | 1 | 0 | 0 | n.d. | n.d. | n.d. | n.d. | n.d. | n.d. | n.d. |
| 80 | web page | 1 | 1 | 1 | 1 | 0 | 1 | 0 | 0 | n.d. | n.d. | n.d. | n.d. | n.d. | n.d. | n.d. |
| 81 | web page | 1 | 0 | 1 | 0 | 0 | 0 | 3 | 1 | n.d. | n.d. | n.d. | n.d. | n.d. | n.d. | n.d. |
| **Mean** | | 0.72 | 0.37 | 0.26 | 0.47 | 0.26 | 0.53 | 8.71 | 6.15 | 3.27 | 3.41 | 3.88 | 4.27 | 4.18 | 4.48 | 4.67 |
| **Variance** | | 0.21 | 0.24 | 0.19 | 0.25 | 0.19 | 0.25 | 60,1 | 43,9 | 2.20 | 1.94 | 1.40 | 1.19 | 1.47 | 0.68 | 0.53 |

*Tab. 4 Grouped Results*

| | interviews | e-mail | web page | |
|---|---|---|---|---|
| | 41 | 25 | 16 | 82 |
| Question | access | no access | | |
| 1. | 59 | 23 | | 82 |
| in % | 72% | 28% | | |
| 2. | 26 | 4 | | |
| in % | 44% | 17% | | |
| 3.a | 15 | 7 | | |
| in % | 25% | 30% | | |
| 3.b | 29 | 9 | | |
| in % | 49% | 39% | | |
| 3.c | 10 | 11 | | |
| in % | 17% | 48% | | |
| 3.d | 30 | 13 | | |
| in % | 51% | 57% | | |

# Appendix C: Internet-User in Europe

**Internet-User in Europe**

*Tab. 5  Internet-User in Europe*

| Country | Date | Online-user | Penetration |
|---|---|---:|---:|
| Austria | Aug 98 | 442,000 | 5,5% |
| Belgium | Feb 99 | 1,400,000 | 16.0% |
| Denmark | Nov 98 | 1,100,000 | 22.0% |
| Estonia | July 97 | 8,280 | 1.8% |
| Finland | Aug 98 | 1,430,000 | 27.9% |
| France | May 98 | 2,500,000 | 5.2% |
| Germany | Mar 98 | 8,400,000 | 9.6% |
| Greece | Jan 98 | 111,000 | 1.0% |
| Hungry | Mai 98 | 2000,000 | 2.0% |
| Ireland | Oct 98 | 300,000 | 11.0% |
| Island | Dec 98 | 121,074 | 45.0% |
| Italy | May 98 | 2,600,000 | 4.1% |
| Netherlands | Nov 98 | 1,800,000 | 10.7% |
| Norway | Jan 98 | 601,000 | 13.6% |
| Portugal | Jan 98 | 188,000 | 1.9% |
| Russia | Jul 98 | 1,000,000 | 0.67% |
| Sweden | Nov 98 | 2,9000,000 | 33.0% |
| Switzerland | Sept 98 | 1,200,000 | 16.2% |
| Slovakia | Sept 98 | 510,000 | 9.5% |
| Spain | Oct 98 | 2,247,000 | 6.6% |
| Turkey | May 97 | 600,000 | 1.0% |

source: [FOC99]

**Diplomarbeiten** Agentur

Die Diplomarbeiten Agentur vermarktet seit 1996 erfolgreich
Wirtschaftsstudien, Diplomarbeiten, Magisterarbeiten, Dissertationen
und andere Studienabschlußarbeiten aller Fachbereiche und Hochschulen.

**Seriosität, Professionalität und Exklusivität prägen unsere Leistungen:**
- Kostenlose Aufnahme der Arbeiten in unser Lieferprogramm
- Faire Beteiligung an den Verkaufserlösen
- Autorinnen und Autoren können den Verkaufspreis selber festlegen
- Effizientes Marketing über viele Distributionskanäle
- Präsenz im Internet unter **http://www.diplom.de**
- Umfangreiches Angebot von mehreren tausend Arbeiten
- Großer Bekanntheitsgrad durch Fernsehen, Hörfunk und Printmedien

Setzen Sie sich mit uns in Verbindung:

**Diplomarbeiten** Agentur
Dipl. Kfm. Dipl. Hdl. Björn Bedey —
Dipl. Wi.-Ing. Martin Haschke ——
und Guido Meyer GbR ————

Hermannstal 119 k ————
22119 Hamburg ————

Fon: 040 / 655 99 20 ————
Fax: 040 / 655 99 222 ————

agentur@diplom.de ————
www.diplom.de ————

www.ingramcontent.com/pod-product-compliance
Lightning Source LLC
La Vergne TN
LVHW092341060326
832902LV00008B/763